Dance
LIKE DAVID DANCED

Discovering Dance in the Bible
& Dance Ministry for God's Glory

CARLA J. PEREZ

Dance Like David Danced:
Discovering Dance in the Bible &
Dance Ministry for God's Glory
By Carla J. Perez © Copyright 2022

Unless otherwise specified, scriptures used throughout the book are from the Tree of Life (TLV) Translation of the Bible. Copyright © 2015 by The Messianic Jewish Family Bible Society. Used by permission.

This version uses some Jewish terms in place of English words, such as the title Yeshua instead of Jesus. A glossary of Hebrew/Aramaic words, with their English counterparts, is included in the Appendix to help your understanding of words that may be unfamiliar.

The chapters of this book progress through the mentions of dance in the order they appear in the Bible. However, the order of the books in the TLV Bible varies slightly from other versions. In the Old Testament, *The Writings*, which include Psalms, Proverbs, Job, and other books, are separated from and follow the books of *The Prophets.*

You will find that some of the verse numbers, especially in the book of Psalms and Song of Songs, will not match the Bible versions you may be more familiar with. For example, the first verse in the TLV, is often the explanation or title that in other versions is not numbered. So, if you look up a verse in another version that doesn't correspond to the text of this book, simply jump back one or two verses.

Throughout this book, the spelling of the word *halleluyah*, reflects the Hebrew spelling rather than the English or Latin version, *hallelujah*.

In keeping with the design of the TLV Bible, the name *satan,* the accuser of man, is purposefully not capitalized.

Scripture quotations marked (KJV) are taken from the Holy Bible, King James Version (Public Domain).

Cover and Interior Design by Exodus Design
www.ExodusDesign.com

Edited by Donna Ferrier
www.ChristianEditorWorldwide.com

ISBN: 9798987697504

Printed in U.S.A.

First Edition

Dedication

To the Lord, my God, I give all glory and praise.
He has brought me out of my pit and
set my feet on a firm foundation.
This is His book, a portion of His story,
spoken through me.

Also to the reader, the dancer in you,
I bless you and cheer you on.

Acknowledgments

Special thanks to my husband, Michael Perez. Without your blessing and support this book could not have come about.

Thank you, Pastors Jack and Lynnett Serr; and my mother Sharon Loy, for continually encouraging and cheering me on in my dance.

Many thanks and appreciation to the ministries that have directly influenced my ministry: Mary Lindow, Castlewood Canyon Church, Called to Flag, Joanne's Dance Studio, and Christ Center for Dance.

Thank you, Cindy Barker and Stephanie Schureman, for listening, sharing wisdom, advice, and offering prayer in the development stages of my writing.

Much gratitude goes to all those that have surrounded and touched my life. Whether in long-term relationships, or brief encounters, each one of you has helped shape who I am today. There are too many to specifically list, but I thank you for your friendship, prayers, and spiritual encouragement.

Contents

Part Two: God's Inexhaustible Word

Part Three: Dancing for the Lord

Appendix

Preface

When the Lord called me to dance, I had no idea what He was leading me into or even the first steps to take. I had no formal dance background or training. I had only experienced dance as a fun and social activity through school dances, Friday night dances, and dancing at concerts. I met my husband one evening when he asked me for a dance, and I danced with my children as they grew.

From Bible stories and teachings, I had heard of Miriam's dance, David's dance, and somehow, somewhere along my path, I came to believe that Queen Vashti in the book of Esther was deposed of her position because she refused to dance—appropriately or inappropriately—for King Ahasuerus and his banquet guests (which is probably not true as dance is never mentioned in the book of Esther).

So, how did the Lord want me to dance for Him? He was about to teach me, but first I had to go through a process of healing, learning to listen and trust, becoming sensitive to His Spirit, knowing His Word, and walking by faith rather than by sight.

As I studied dance from a biblical perspective and grew in my relationship with the Lord, He led me to write this book sharing what His Word says about dance. As you read this book, my desire is that you will discover God's heart for dance as something good, something joyful, something pleasing for Him as well as for us.

Dancing comes natural to us; most cultures have expressions of dance. In fact, it has to be taught as something evil, wicked, and sinful in order to prevent it. That is not God's intention, but a tactic of the enemy to destroy what He has created and blessed.

May you find peace, wisdom, understanding, and joy as you discover God's heart for dance, and may you end up dancing as David danced.

Introduction

*"I am the Alpha and the Omega, the First and the Last,
the Beginning and the End."*
—Revelation 22:13

The Lord God Almighty is the Creator and Author of all things, the First and the Last, and the Giver of good gifts, having created all things for His glory. You are part of that creation. He thought of you, designed your specific DNA, and placed an eternal spirit within you. You exist because God chose to breathe life into you. Do you wonder why He created you and why you exist?

The word *will* in Revelation 4:11 means "pleasure." It comes from the Greek word *thélēma* (thel'-ay-mah), which means "a determination such as an active choice or a passive inclination: desire, pleasure, will." He created you for His pleasure! He delights in you. Check out these verses about created things:

*All things were made through Him, and apart from Him
nothing was made that has come into being.*
—John 1:3

*Then God said, "Let Us make man in Our image,
after Our likeness!"*
—Genesis 1:26a

*Then ADONAI Elohim formed the man out of the dust
from the ground and He breathed into his nostrils a
breath of life—so the man became a living being.*
—Genesis 2:7

But how do we truly know from these verses why we are here?
What is my specific purpose? What is yours? In the Old Testament,
Jeremiah was a young prophet who struggled with God's purpose
for him and God's specific call on his life. Read what God said to
Jeremiah in response to his doubt:

*"Before I formed you in the womb, I knew you, and be-
fore you were born, I set you apart—I appointed you
prophet to the nations."*
—Jeremiah 1:5

God's Word is good and complete. Like Jeremiah, you have
also been known and appointed by God for something specific and
good. Scripture confirms it, and that is how we begin to know the
answers to the questions of purpose and calling.

*Your eyes saw me when I was unformed, and in Your
book were written the days that were formed—when not
one of them had come to be. How precious are Your
thoughts, O God! How great is the sum of them!*
—Psalm 139:16–17

*For we are His workmanship—created in Messiah Ye-
shua for good deeds, which God prepared beforehand so
we might walk in them.*
—Ephesians 2:10

He created you in His image, for His pleasure, because of His will. You are a three-part being. You have a spirit; a soul (mind, will, and emotions); and a physical body. God creates things for beauty and glory. He created you, desiring that you would choose Him and have an intimate, glorious, beautiful, productive relationship with Him. He has blessed you with all the good things you need for this life, and He has prepared good things for you to do, the most important being to share His good news, His gospel message, with others. Maybe He created you to do that through dance.

Get ready to discover God's heart regarding dance. *Dance Like David Danced* covers every mention of dance in the Bible. In its simplest form, dance is movement, usually to music or to a rhythmic beat. It is a response, often an emotional one, to sounds and vibrations in the atmosphere, or even a response to the source or communicator of that sound.

I hope you will study this book with your favorite Bible at your side. Let yourself be taken into the events surrounding each dance, imagining you are there as things take place. Take in the expressed thoughts of the hearts and souls of those who lived long ago, and envision what you would have done if you had been directly involved in the dancing. Dig into the history of dance and grow in your understanding of it in biblical times as you discover the resulting blessings or consequences of each dance. Learn what led to each dance, get to know the parties involved, and discover God's heart toward His dancing ones. Gain a deeper knowledge of God's Word as you learn bits of the original Hebrew, Aramaic, or Greek text.

Take time at the end of each chapter to draw near to God. Speak to Him about the scriptures. Bless Him, praise Him, repent if you need to, and receive His love and wisdom for your life. Open your heart and mind to the depth of God's love for, and approval of, you and your personal dance.

> *For from Him and through Him and to Him are all*
> *things. To Him be the glory forever. Amen.*
> *—Romans 11:36*

May Holy Spirit be with you as you journey through this book. May your relationship with the Lord be strengthened, and may you step out and dance boldly for your Savior and King. Dance as David danced.

PART ONE
Biblical Dance

– 1 –

A Dance of Rejoicing

Then Miriam the prophetess, Aaron's sister, took a
tambourine in her hand, and all the women went out
after her with tambourines and with dancing,
as Miriam sang to them: Sing to ADONAI,
for He is highly exalted! The horse and
its rider He has thrown into the sea!
—Exodus 15:20–21

The first mention of dance in the Bible is Miriam's dance of rejoicing. The full story surrounding Miriam's dance is found in Exodus 14–15.

Miriam grew up in a Hebrew slave family in Egypt and played a large role in the life of her brother Moses. The children of Israel greatly increased in number during their time of slavery to the Egyptians. Pharaoh, the king of Egypt, sought to control their growth by increased labor and cruelty toward them. However, they continued to multiply. Pharaoh feared that if war broke out, the Hebrews could join his enemies, fight against him, and escape from the land. His solution was to command the midwives to kill all Hebrew baby boys at birth, thereby reducing their population and strength. Miriam's brother Moses was born. Scripture describes the baby as "desirable," "goodly," and "extraordinarily beautiful" (Exodus 2:2 and Acts 7:20), so Moses' mother, Jochebed, hid him for three months. When hiding him was no longer feasible, Jochebed placed him in a basket and set him in the Nile River.

Miriam watched and followed the floating basket with her baby brother crying inside until it came to where Pharaoh's daughter was bathing at the riverside. Moved by compassion for the baby, the princess decided to keep him as her own. Here is where Miriam intervened and offered to find him a nurse maid, who of course turned out to be his own mother. Miriam had the intelligence and confidence to follow Moses down the river and then boldly speak to Pharaoh's daughter; an indication that she was not a small child.

Time carried on. After weaning, Moses was raised in Pharaoh's house, always aware that he had a Hebrew heritage. One day, Moses observed an Egyptian severely mistreat his people. Assuming no one would see him, Moses killed the Egyptian and hid him in the sand. However, his kinsmen had observed the actions and did not appreciate his attempted intervention. Fearing that Pharaoh would discover his act, he fled to the land of Midian where he settled and married; had two children; and spent the next forty years shepherding flocks for his father-in-law Jethro.

The Lord heard the groanings from Moses' people, still enslaved in Egypt while Moses was away, and the time became ripe to send him back to help release them from bondage. God spoke to Moses through a burning bush that was not consumed by the fire, telling him to return to Pharaoh for their release. Now wouldn't that get your attention? Reluctantly, but with God's promise to send Moses' brother, Aaron, to assist him, and the promise that He would deliver His people through Moses' actions of obedience to the Lord, Moses returned to Egypt to confront Pharaoh for their release.

Instead of circumstances getting better for the Hebrews once Moses returned, they got worse. Much worse. With each demand from Moses for their freedom, Pharaoh increased their workload and abuses, and many of them resented Moses for coming to free them.

Obedient to the voice of the Lord rather than man, Moses pressed on for their release to go and worship God. During this time, God sent the promised plagues in response to Pharaoh's stubborn heart and refusals. Only following the tenth plague, the death of the firstborn of all living things (including Pharaoh's son), was Pharaoh finally willing to release the Hebrews. Now, he wanted them gone, and gone immediately.

Having already prepared for this according to God's directives, the masses of Hebrew people, along with others who chose to join them, made their way out of Egypt. So fearful of what had happened, and eager to see the Hebrews quickly leave, the Egyptians gladly and generously gave whatever the Hebrews asked for. They plundered the Egyptians of their silver, gold, and clothing.

After a bit of time, however, Pharaoh recanted on their release and sent his armies to chase after them, catching up to them at the Sea of Reeds. Trapped at the water's edge, the Hebrews once again feared for their lives. Directed by his ever-faithful God, Moses stretched out his hand over the sea and the Lord parted the waters so they could cross. As the Egyptians also tried to cross, however, the water came back over them and destroyed the entire army.

Seeing the Lord had saved them, Moses and Miriam broke out singing and praising God for His demonstration of absolute greatness and power in freeing them and their people. Astounded over this miracle, they sang a new song with music birthed from their rejoicing hearts. Following Miriam's lead, "all the women went out after her with tambourines and with dancing."

Moses' and Miriam's song, as well as Miriam's dance with the women, were spontaneous acts of praise and worship in response to God's love and saving grace that He had just poured out for them. The words of their song declared what had just transpired by God's mighty hand. Miriam's dance was a deep emotional response, an ecstatic reaction—rejoicing with wisdom, understanding, and exultation—to what the Lord had just miraculously done. There was no preparation, just praise springing forth from their mouths and their very beings. This is a wonderful way to worship God.

Rejoice in the Lord always—again I will say, rejoice!
—Philippians 4:4

While Miriam's dance is the first mention of dance in the Bible, was it the birthing of dance on the earth? Picture the Garden of Eden, the most beautiful place that has ever existed, lush and fertile and full of the broad spectrum of the plant and animal kingdoms and their musical speech just before God's final creation.

Then God created His final glory: man, or Adam. Seeing that Adam was alone, God caused him to fall into a deep sleep while He formed a perfect partner for him from his own side. Now creation was complete, and not only *good*, but *very good*.

Imagine the Lord walking and speaking His pleasure with Adam and Eve in the cool of the evening. Was there some form of music and dance there when they were perfectly free, amazed by the goodness of their Creator and the beauty of the garden they inhabited? God gave a hint of an answer when He spoke in the book of Job.

> *"Where were you… when the morning stars sang*
> *together, and all the sons of God shouted for joy?"*
> —*Job 38:4, 7*

Another hint of an answer is found in the book of John.

> *All things were made through Him, and apart from Him*
> *nothing was made that has come into being.*
> —*John 1:3*

God created all things including music and our response to music; dance. So, no, Miriam's dancing was not the first dance on earth. But dancing is something that pleased the Lord to put within us from the start.

Exodus 7:7 tells us that "Moses was eighty years old, and Aaron eighty-three years old when they spoke to Pharaoh." This indicates that Miriam, being older than Moses and Aaron, may have been in her late 80's or even in her 90's when she led the other women in song and dance to the Lord. God's children are never too old to worship Him in dance. Regardless of age, stepping out in faith and action when led by the Holy Spirit will draw others to join in, rejoicing and praising the Lord.

When something miraculous happens in your life, your family, or your church family, be free to dance and sing to the Lord.

Sing to ADONAI a new song!
Sing to ADONAI, all the earth.
Sing to ADONAI, bless His Name.
Proclaim the good news of
His salvation from day to day.
Declare His glory among the nations,
His marvelous deeds among all peoples.
For great is ADONAI, and greatly to be praised.
He is to be feared above all gods.
—Psalm 96:1–4

– 2 –

Dances of Revelry

*Then it happened, as soon as Moses came near the camp,
he saw the calf and the dancing, and his anger burned
hot. So he threw the tablets out of his hands, and
smashed them at the foot of the mountain. Then he took
the calf that they had made, burned it with fire, ground
it to powder, scattered it on the surface of the water and
made Bnei-Yisrael drink it.*
—Exodus 32:19–20

Seventeen chapters after the glorious rejoicing of Miriam's dance, the children of Israel are dancing again. This time, however, the rejoicing was not to the Lord, but to themselves for what they thoughtlessly and wickedly created—a golden calf as their god in place of the Lord Most High who had just brought them out of Egypt. How could they do such a thing after the Lord had just parted the Red Sea to deliver them from an enemy bent on their enslavement?

The Hebrews had been slaves for 400 years, or 4 generations, according to Genesis 15:16. During that time, Pharaoh provided supplies for the slaves' brick-making work until Moses came along. But because of Moses' intervention, Pharaoh increased the labor and reduced the provisions for their work, which made life frustratingly more difficult, causing many to become bitter and callous toward Moses.

Once the children of Israel were released from Egypt and out on their own, Exodus 16–32 provides details of their grumblings, continued miraculous provisions, in-fighting, and war as they learned to rely on the Lord instead of Pharaoh. While the Israelites obviously knew about their God, it was only head knowledge and not experiential knowledge. During the 400 years of slavery, God had been silent toward them until Moses encountered Him at the burning bush. While the Israelites desired freedom, they did not know how to manage it.

When a person is set free from a dysfunctional environment, he or she may feel an immediate sense of relief, freedom, and a desire to live differently from that point forward. But without continual guidance, that person will fall back into what is familiar, namely the dysfunctional behaviors and relationships. Transformation often takes tremendous effort and time.

Moving from a childhood home for the first time, young adults generally experience a period of independent revelry. They test the truths or untruths of their upbringing and often try participating in activities that had been unapproved or forbidden. With time and wisdom, they once again settle into reliable patterns of living.

Imagine the vast number of Israelites suddenly released from their dysfunctional existence into total freedom and self-reliance. While the Hebrews remained relatively untouched as God poured out plagues on the Egyptians, their journey out of the country was not exactly filled with comfort and constant provision. On the contrary, they were in for a rude awakening.

Instead of relying on Pharaoh for their work, food, and shelter, the Lord wanted them to trust and rely on Him. Moses, their "brother" who was raised in an Egyptian household, and who ran away for forty years, would now be the one who would lead them. But even after the miraculous parting of the Red Sea, the Israelites grumbled against Moses because they lacked water, meat, and bread. So, Moses and Aaron sought the Lord for them, and they received water, turned from bitter to sweet; meat each evening; and manna (a bread-like substance) from heaven each morning (Exodus 15:22–16:36).

As they journeyed further, they continued complaining about the lack of water, and God taught Moses to listen carefully and obey His voice no matter how foolish the instructions may have sounded. God provided water from a rock, victory in wars against enemies, and wisdom through Moses' father-in-law in learning how to manage vast numbers of people. ADONAI continually showed His people that He was for them and not against them (Exodus 17–18).

Three months into their wilderness journey, the Israelites arrived at Sinai. Just as we often do not know what lies ahead of us, they too had no idea what God was about to do. God is a good, good Father. He knew His children needed to know how to successfully live freely. So, God called Moses up the mountain to meet with Him and give him these instructions to give to the people.

> *Now then, if you listen closely to My voice, and keep*
> *My covenant, then you will be My own treasure from*
> *among all people, for all the earth is Mine.*
> *—Exodus 19:5*

Moses doesn't climb Sinai to be with God just once, but multiple times. The next time you read Exodus 19–32, count the number of times Moses went up and then down. He must have been in pretty good shape with all the walking and climbing he did.

The Israelites got a little impatient with Moses' trips to meet with God. They didn't fully grasp that Moses' many and long meetings with God on the mountaintop were for their good. God was laying the framework for living a holy, good, abundant life. God gave Moses the Ten Commandments, rules about healthy relationships and living in harmony with one another. He also gave Moses incredible details for making the first tabernacle, and instructions for ministering to Him through the holy covenant. Everything was to be done with great attention. The Tabernacle, the ministry clothing, and the articles of service, were all to be skillfully and exquisitely created.

Unfortunately, when the Israelites finally got tired of waiting for Moses to come down the mountain, they took matters into their own hands. They talked Aaron into making a golden calf, declaring it was their god that had brought them out of Egypt. They figured if handmade gods of gold prospered the Egyptians, those gods should work for them as well.

> *They rose up early the next morning, sacrificed burnt offerings and brought fellowship offerings. The people sat down to eat and drink, and rose up to make merry.*
> —*Exodus 32:6*

> *Then it happened, as soon as Moses came near the camp, he saw the calf and the dancing, and his anger burned hot.*
> —*Exodus 32:19a*

*…Moses saw that the people were unrestrained, because
Aaron had let them run wild, to become a joke
among their enemies…*
—*Exodus 32:25*

*So the sons of Levi did as Moses said, and that day from
among the people there fell about 3,000 men.*
—*Exodus 32:28*

God had done so much for His children, and they repaid Him by reverting to unrestrained licentious behavior and worshiping a manmade image. God called the people stiff-necked and He wanted to consume them in His burning hot wrath against them (Exodus 32:9). In Exodus 32:30 Moses called their actions "a horrendous sin."

The sinful self-serving dances of merry-making and revelry greatly displeased God and brought much heartache and grief to the One who had created and loved them, as well as death and dishonor to many of the people. Many people still dance this way today, unwittingly serving other gods for their own pleasures.

Does God's reaction seem a bit harsh to you? It helps to understand who He is. He is pure love. He is holy. He is sinless. There is no evil in Him, nor can He tolerate it. When Adam and Eve brought sin into the world, everything changed. Directly communing with God became impossible. Atoning, or covering for sin so the Lord could continue guiding man required a blood sacrifice. But the blood of animals was not enough to free mankind from sin; it only "covered" it.

In time, again out of pure love, God sent His Only Son for us. Because of the perfect sacrifice of Jesus Christ for the sins of humanity, the Lord now patiently waits for all who will repent of their sinful behaviors and turn to Him, not wanting anyone to perish. Thankfully, the patience of God in our lives means salvation for many (2 Peter 3:15a).

The Lord is not slow in keeping His promise, as some
consider slowness. Rather, He is being patient toward
you—not wanting anyone to perish,
but for all to come to repentance.
—2 Peter 3:9

Remember not the sins of my youth, nor my rebellion.
According to Your mercy remember me, for the sake
of Your goodness, ADONAI.
—Psalm 25:7

Do you have a loved one in your life who seems so far from the Lord as he or she lives life oblivious to any higher power other than their self? Maybe you have friends and family who follow other religions and traditions. Maybe that person is you. The Lord is patient and longsuffering toward everyone. He will never force anyone to choose Him, but He will lovingly continue to bless them, desiring that they will see and know His goodness.

…He causes His sun to rise on the evil and the good,
and sends rain on the righteous
and the unrighteous.
—Matthew 5:45

Keep praying and believing for those currently lost in the world's ways to turn to the Lord. What seems impossible with man is possible with God (Matthew 19:26).

– 3 –

The Dance of Devastation

Now when Jephthah arrived at his home in Mizpah, be-
hold, his daughter was coming out to meet him with
tambourines and with dances. Now she was his only
child. Besides her he had no son or daughter.
—Judges 11:34

The dance of Jephthah's daughter is probably the most sorrowful dance in the Bible. It is difficult to fully comprehend what happened here. Jephthah was an illegitimate child, the son of his father, Gilead, and a prostitute (Gileadites were from the tribe of Manasseh, Gilead being Manasseh's grandson, Numbers 26:29–30). Gilead had other sons by his lawful wife. The sons of his wife eventually drove Jephthah away, declaring they would not share any of their father's inheritance with him. He fled and lived in the land of Tob.

The very first thing mentioned of Jephthah, even before explaining his lineage, is that he was a mighty man of valor (Judges 11:1). The word *valor* means to exhibit great courage in the face of danger, especially in battle. In an effort to regain possession of the land, the children of Ammon came to fight against Israel. Suddenly, the mighty Israelite Jephthah was of great value in the eyes of Gilead's elders. They sought him out and asked him to be their chief in the fight and even offered him the right to become their leader if he'd agree. He must have been one tough and scary dude for the Gileadites to think he was the only way to win this battle.

Jephthah was also knowledgeable about Israel's history, which is evident from his exchange of words with the king of Ammon as he tried to persuade him to back down from his intent to go to war over the possession of the land God had given the Israelites (Judges 11:14–27). But the Ammonite king paid no attention to Jephthah's wise words.

> *Then the Ruach ADONAI came upon Jephthah, so he marched through Gilead and Manasseh, and passed through Mizpah of Gilead, and from Mizpah of Gilead he crossed over to the children of Ammon.*
> *—Judges 11:29*

Indeed, Jephthah was a mighty man of valor. By the power of God's Spirit upon him, he boldly marched to confront the king of Ammon and his children. However, in his boldness, Jephthah made a horribly rash vow.

> *Then Jephthah vowed a vow to ADONAI and said, "If You will indeed give the children of Ammon into my hand, then it will be that whatever comes out of the doors of my house to meet me when I return safely from the children of Ammon, it will be ADONAI'S, and I will offer it up as a burnt offering.*
> *—Judges 11:30–31*

Hadn't the Lord already given this land to the children of Israel (Numbers 21:21–35)? Would He not give them success since He had previously driven out the inhabitants for them? Instead of humbly seeking God for favor, Jephthah made this rash vow. It seems he may have been overconfident in the moment and blurted out these words. Did he have pets inside his home that he thought would be the first to run out when the door was opened, or servants perhaps? It is so very difficult to think he was willing to sacrifice a servant or a family member in exchange for this victory. He was a knowledgeable man. He knew the Law required him to keep a vow made to the Lord (Numbers 30:2, Deuteronomy 23:24).

The Lord answered his request and gave him victory over the Ammonites. Word must have spread while the army plundered and celebrated on their return home. Seeing him arriving, his daughter joyfully danced out of the house to greet him. Oh, how he was grieved when he saw her coming out so full of life, joy, and pride, dancing and rejoicing over her father's great success. This must have been a father who adored his daughter that she would so freely celebrate his victorious return.

But her joy did not last long. Seeing his distressed reaction of tearing his garments, she then hears her father's anguished explanation of the reckless vow he had made. Her response is just as incredulous as his rash vow. Honoring her father and the Lord, she graciously accepted her fate "since ADONAI brought vengeance on your enemies" (Judges 11:36). She only asked that she be given some time in the mountains with her friends to mourn because of her virginity. After two months, she returned, and her father performed his vow (Judges 11:39).

How do we deal with the thoughts and emotions over this blip of history? It was important enough to include in the Word so we could learn from it, so what are we to learn? Considering the time we are now in, following the sacrifice of our Lord Jesus Christ for our sins, we can be ever so grateful that He does not hold us to perfect obedience to the Law. God, through Jesus Christ, has "walked in our shoes." He knows what is in a man, understands our weaknesses, and has forgiven all our sins, including our own thoughtless statements. Consequences for our thoughts and actions still apply, however. We must, therefore, continue to grow and mature in our thoughts and behaviors to safeguard ourselves as well as others. Words and declarations carry significance and weight.

> *Death and life are in the control of the tongue. Those*
> *who indulge in it will eat its fruit.*
> *—Proverbs 18:21*

> *He who watches his mouth protects his life, but whoever*
> *opens wide his lips comes to ruin.*
> *—Proverbs 13:3*

> *Whoever guards his mouth and tongue keeps his soul*
> *out of troubles.*
> *—Proverbs 21:23*

> *Set a guard, ADONAI, over my mouth. Keep watch*
> *over the door of my lips.*
> *—Psalm 141:3*

What seemed as though it were going to be a triumphant story ends tragically. Yet God is always full of love and grace toward all. While He does not remove the consequences of our choices, we can humbly come to Him seeking forgiveness. He is forever gracious to quickly forgive, accept and restore us to Himself. What a mighty God we serve.

$$- 4 -$$

Dances of Shiloh

"And watch, and behold, if the daughters of Shiloh
should come out to join in the dances, then come
out of the vineyards, and let each of you catch
his wife from among the daughters of Shiloh.
Then go to the land of Benjamin."
—Judges 21:21

So the children of Benjamin did so, and took the number
of wives from the dancers whom they carried off. Then
they went and returned to their inheritance, and rebuilt
the towns and settled in them.
—Judges 21:23

Most people celebrate some form of annual feasts. Christians celebrate Easter and Christmas in particular. If you are Jewish, maybe you celebrate the Messianic or Jewish feasts. Maybe you celebrate annual birthdays with parties, food, and games. Is joyful dancing ever a part of these events?

Judges 21:19 refers to "the feast of ADONAI" at which the daughters of Shiloh, in verse twenty-one, might "come out to join in the dances." God commanded Moses to celebrate several feasts, so which feast is verse nineteen referring to that includes dancing? Why was there some question as to whether the daughters would come out or not?

Annual feasts and harvest feasts are mentioned in Exodus 23, Leviticus 23, and Deuteronomy 16. In addition to honoring the Sabbath, Leviticus 23 specifically outlines seven separate feasts of the Lord that required sacred assemblies: Passover, Unleavened Bread, Firstfruits, Feast of Weeks, Feast of Trumpets, Day of Atonement, and Feast of Tabernacles.

While the biblical text does not specify which specific feast was being held in Judges 21, scholars point to either the Spring Feast of Passover or the Fall Feast of Tabernacles. I personally lean toward the Feast of Tabernacles because scripture indicates that this was a more festive and joyful feast. Regarding this feast, Leviticus 23:40 says the people are to "rejoice before Adonai," and verse forty-one mentions twice "you are to celebrate."

The Hebrew word for *rejoice* is *sâmach* (saw-makh') which means to brighten up or be gleesome. It's usually a spontaneous emotion or extreme happiness that is sometimes accompanied by dancing, and singing as at a feast or festival. The Hebrew word for *celebrate* is *châgag* (khaw-gag'), which means to move in a circle, to march in a sacred procession, to observe a festival; or to be giddy (celebrate, dance, keep, or hold a solemn feast or holiday, reel to and fro).

Also in Judges 21:21, we read that each of the men would "catch" his wife. The original word for *catch* is *châtaph* (khaw-taf'), which means to clutch or basically to seize as a prisoner. So the plan was that each man would capture a woman to be his wife. Now the daughters did not know of this plan, so to answer the question, "Why were the daughters hesitant to come out?" we need to go back to the mortifying story that unfolds in Judges 19.

People who resided in Shiloh were of the tribe of Ephraim. Shiloh was between Bethel and Shechem (Bethel to the south in the land of the tribe of Benjamin, and Shechem to the north in the land of the tribe of Manasseh). A Levite priest from the land of Ephraim had taken a concubine from Bethlehem in Judah (south of the land of Benjamin). She demonstrated unfaithfulness to him by going back to her father's house, where she stayed for four months.

The Levite decided to go to her and speak kindly to her. He took along a servant and donkeys and traveled south from Ephraim through Benjamin to the northern part of Judah. He stayed for several days in her father's home, and it seems her father enjoyed his company because each day he asked the Levite to stay another day to eat, drink, and be merry.

The priest, concubine, and servants finally headed on their journey home, stopping to rest for a night at Gibeah in the land of Benjamin. An old man, an Ephraimite who lived in Gibeah, was returning to town from a day's work and noticed the Levite and his company in the town square. So he invited them to his home to feed them and give them a place to sleep for the night.

Unsavory men from the town had noticed the Levite being taken in. They went to the house and demanded the old man bring him out so they could have relations with him. After much arguing and pleading, the old man gave the wicked men his virgin daughter and the Levite's concubine to abuse.

When morning came, the Levite gathered his belongings to leave. Outside the doorstep he found his concubine, who had made her way back to the house and had died from the trauma of being abused by the wicked men. The Levite put her on one of the donkeys, returned home, and then proceeded to cut his concubine into twelve pieces, delivering one piece to each of the territories of Israel.

Upon hearing about the obscene and degrading event that took place within the land of Israel, the incensed leaders assembled 400,000 foot soldiers to go to war against Benjamin. They intended to put the wicked men to death, but the Benjamites refused to turn them over to the leaders. Instead, the men of Benjamin gathered the men of Gibeah and another 26,000 swordsmen from the surrounding area. Of these men, 700 were left-handed, which provided an advantage of skill and an element of surprise against a greater number of right-handed opponents. The Benjamites struck down 22,000 Israelites on the first day of the battle, and 18,000 the second day.

The children of Israel who had inquired of the Lord regarding these battles were distraught over their losses and withdrew to Bethel in the northern part of Benjamin. They fasted, offered sacrifices, and sought the Lord again as to whether they should go out against Benjamin, their brother-tribe, or cease the fighting. The Lord told them to go, for He would give them success this time.

So they set an ambush against Benjamin and killed 25,100 that day. Six hundred men of Benjamin—less than 2.5 percent of the original number of men—turned and escaped into the wilderness. They hid for four months while the Israelites went back through the land, killed everyone and everything that was still alive, and burned down the towns.

The Israelites were grieved over the sin and devastating loss of their brother-tribe. Some of the Benjamites escaped the wrath, but how would they rebuild their tribe with only 600 men? You see, in Judges 21:7, the men of Israel had taken an oath declaring they would not give any of their daughters in marriage to the Benjamites. The Lord considered this oath sacred, so they could not go back on what they spoke.

During the planning of the attack, the men of Israel had taken another solemn oath that anyone who failed to come together in their effort against Benjamin would also be put to death. As the leaders accounted for the tribes that had assembled, they discovered that no one from the town of Jabesh Gilead had come. So 12,000 of Israel's valiant warriors were sent out to slay the men and any woman among them who had lain with a man. They found 400 of the women to be virgins, whom they took back to their camp at Shiloh and gave to the men of Benjamin to be their wives. That still left 200 men without wives.

They remembered the annual feast of the Lord that was held in Shiloh and commanded the remaining men to hide in the vineyards to see if the daughters of Shiloh would join in the dances. Aware of the horrible event of the Levite priest and his concubine, the daughters may have been hesitant to attend the dances. But if they came out to dance, then the men could come out from hiding, and each of them could catch a woman to be his wife. In this way, no one was "giving" daughters to this tribe; the men simply carried them off. So they did as planned, returned home, and the Benjamites were then able to rebuild.

The final verse, Judges 21:25, explains quite a bit: "In those days there was no king in Israel. Everyone did what was right in his own eyes."

What a terrible mess these brother-tribes found themselves in. Despite the terrible events, God used the annual festival to the

Lord and the dancing daughters at Shiloh to bring about undeserved restoration and redemption. He was merciful toward Israel, and He remains the same toward us today.

> *He has not treated us according to our sins, or repaid us*
> *according to our iniquities. For as high as the heavens*
> *are above the earth, so great is His mercy for*
> *those who fear Him.*
> *—Psalm 103:10–11*

Merciful indeed.

– 5 –

Victory Dances

*Upon their coming back, upon David's return from kill-
ing the Philistine, the women came out of all the towns
of Israel, singing and dancing in circles to greet King
Saul, with timbrels, with joy and with three-stringed
instruments. So the women sang one to another, as
they were dancing saying, "Saul has slain his
thousands, and David his ten thousands!"*
—1 Samuel 18:6–7

*But Achish's courtiers said to him, "Isn't this David
king of the land? Isn't he the one they sing about in
their dances saying, 'Saul has slain his thousands,
and David his ten thousands?'"*
—1 Samuel 21:12

*"Isn't this one David, about whom they were singing in
dances saying: 'Saul has slain his thousands, and David
his ten thousands?'"*
—1 Samuel 29:5

Long before David's famous dancing "with all his might" (2 Samuel 6:14), local women celebrated and honored him with dancing. These must have been exciting celebrations throughout the multiple towns of Israel, which the army passed through on its return from battle.

The children of Israel had decided they wanted a king to rule them, just like all the other nations around them. The prophet, Samuel, warned against this, but the Lord directed him to give them what they desired. God chose Saul as their first anointed and Spirit-filled king.

Saul started off well, but soon began making decisions on his own, not carefully following the Lord's instructions through Samuel the prophet. In one particular battle against the Philistines, recounted in 1 Samuel 13, Saul grew anxious and tired of waiting for Samuel to appear to offer a sacrifice to the Lord before going into battle, so Saul chose to offer the sacrifice himself. As a consequence, the Lord removed His Spirit from Saul and commanded Samuel to anoint a new king.

The Lord sent Samuel to the sons of Jesse and anointed David as king. David was the youngest of all of Jesse's sons, so young in fact that his father didn't include him in his invitation to meet Samuel for a sacrifice to the Lord. Samuel was surprised when God did not reveal any of the seven older sons in attendance as the new king.

> *But ADONAI said to Samuel, "Do not look at his*
> *appearance or his stature, because I have already*
> *refused him. For He does not see a man as man sees,*
> *for man looks at the outward appearance,*
> *but ADONAI looks into the heart."*
> *—1 Samuel 16:7*

"ADONAI has not chosen any of these."
—1 Samuel 16:10b

Samuel pressed Jesse as to whether he had any other sons. He did: his youngest who was out in the fields tending the sheep. They all waited while David was brought in from the field.

Then ADONAI said, "Arise, anoint him, for this is the one." So Samuel took the horn of oil and anointed him in the midst of his brothers. From that day on Ruach ADONAI came mightily upon David.
—1 Samuel 16:12b–13a

Although David was anointed as king, it would be some time before he would take up his reign.

King Saul was in a downward spiral as a result of his own self-righteousness. Without the Holy Spirit, he was now tormented by an evil spirit. Saul's attendants recommended they find someone to play soothing music for the king to help him feel better. One attendant had seen that David, the son of Jesse, was a skilled harpist. Therefore, King Saul's messengers were sent to David's father and requested David's service as an attendant to the king. Now, isn't this beginning to feel a bit awkward? The youth recently anointed to be king is now being sent by his father, along with a donkey, a goat, bread and wine, to serve the king he would eventually replace.

Before Samuel anointed David, 1 Samuel 16:2 reveals that Samuel feared King Saul finding out about him anointing a new king, so the Lord had told him to "sacrifice to ADONAI." Was David told not to reveal his new position when he went to the king? For a youth to keep this information to himself, he had to have been a wise and humble person. As one of Saul's young men, verse eighteen describes David as "a mighty man of valor, a warrior, prudent in speech, a handsome man, and ADONAI is with him."

David became one of Saul's attendants, and Saul loved him. Saul's soul found relief when David played the soothing harp. The king made David one of his armor bearers, and he was highly favored. David ventured back and forth between serving the king and tending his father's flocks (1 Samuel 17:15).

King Saul soon found himself going to battle with the Philistines. Saul and all Israel were terrified of the threats from Goliath, a Philistine giant. David's three oldest brothers were in Saul's army, so his father sent him with food to check on them. While there, he heard the threats of Goliath and was emboldened to inquire what would be done for the man who would strike him down. His bold talk was overheard and reported to Saul. He was then taken to the king.

> *David said to Saul, "Let no one's heart fail because of*
> *him. Your servant will go and fight*
> *with this Philistine."*
> *—1 Samuel 17:32*

Scripture doesn't tell us how much time passed between David's anointing and his service to King Saul, or between the beginning of his service and the battle against the Philistines. In addition to being Jesse's youngest son, and a mighty man of valor, David is described in chapter seventeen as a youth, a ruddy boy, and a young man. Whatever his age, he was confident in the abilities he'd gained while tending his father's sheep, for he had killed lions and bears that rose up against him to save the lambs under his charge.

Saul granted him permission to fight, and David prevailed, slaying Goliath with a sling and a stone. Revealing that their confidence was in Goliath, and not in their collective skill and strength, the Philistines fled the scene, leaving their camp to be plundered by the Israelites. Saul took David with him that day and did not let him return to his father's house. David had success in everything he did for Saul.

Word got around quickly about what had happened in the Philistine battle. There was a lot of celebrating throughout the land of Israel over this victory that didn't look too favorable at the beginning of the battle. As the army returned, passing through towns and villages, the women joyfully came out dancing and singing praises to King Saul. They were much more impressed however with David, and they spread the news of his victory and favor far and wide, bringing distinguished attention to him. This did not sit well with Saul, who took David's praise, or Saul's own lack of praise, very personally. He spent the rest of his years filled with jealousy, repeatedly attempting to take David's life.

There's nothing wrong with celebrating a victory, as long as we wisely remember it is God who gives success. When nations go to war against each other, and one nation is victorious, there is a joyful celebration over the victory; praise for the soldiers who valiantly fought; and respect and honor for those who sacrificed for the people, land, and country.

Think of the world wars we have experienced in the past one hundred years or so. The United States and her allies shouted with joy and danced in the streets in celebration of the brave men who valiantly fought and defeated the enemies. Don't we all enjoy receiving praise for our abilities and accomplishments? Were the women wrong to dance, sing, celebrate, and praise as they did?

No doubt, Saul's selfishness and failure to fully honor and seek God led to his steady decline. It was greatly exacerbated by the women joyously praising David more than they praised him as they celebrated Israel's victory.

Saul's heart had turned from God. In addition, the women sought to exalt David over Saul likely because of his youth, strength, and attractiveness. There is no mention of praising God, who ultimately gives or withholds victory. Some may have praised God, but again, it is not mentioned.

It is through the hand of God toward men that we attain success. Yes, it is good, right, and important to celebrate out victories and bless those who lead the way. Let us also remember that our triumphs come from and through our Heavenly Father, and give Him honor and praise.

With God we will do mighty things,
and He will trample our foes.
—Psalm 60:14

$$- 6 -$$

The Marauders' Dance

*So he led him down, and behold, they were scattered over
all the area, eating, drinking and feasting because of all
the great spoil that they had taken from the land of the
Philistines and from the land of Judah.*
—1 Samuel 30:16

In other translations of the Bible such as the KJV, NLT and Amplified, *feasting*, which is mentioned in 1 Samuel 30:16, is translated as *dancing*. The original Hebrew word used here is *châgag* (khaw-gag'), meaning to move in a circle, (i.e., to march in a sacred procession, to observe a festival, by implication to be giddy). To further understand the intended meaning, let's look at the biblical background.

David had been fleeing from King Saul because he sought to destroy David out of jealousy and to preserve the kingship for his own son. The two had crossed paths a few times, and David, having had an opportunity to harm Saul, refused to do so because it was the Lord who had placed Saul in his position. Saul was "ADONAI's anointed" (1 Samuel 24:6, 26:11, 26:23).

David eventually escaped to Gath in the land of the Philistines, along with 600 of his men, their families, and two of his wives.

When Saul heard where David had fled, Saul stopped pursuing him, possibly because he didn't want another messy encounter with the Philistines. David found favor with Achish, the king of Gath, and the Philistines.

After staying with the king for some time, Achish gave David the town of Ziklag to live in. During this time, David and his men went on raids, taking away goods and livestock, leaving no one alive. This pleased Achish, who thought David had certainly made himself abhorrent to the people of Israel and thus would be his servant forever.

With David now on their side, the Philistines went to battle against Israel again. When a commander of the Philistines noticed David and his men going out to fight with them, he questioned the presence of the Hebrews. Achish defended them, but the commanders grew angry and insisted the Hebrews go back to Ziklag over concern that they would become their adversaries during battle.

David and his men returned to Ziklag and found they had been raided by the Amalekites (enemies of the Israelites whom David had also previously raided). All the inhabitants, including David's two wives, had been taken captive and the town burned with fire. The men grieved deeply and were ready to stone David for their loss, but David was strengthened by the Lord. God confirmed that he and his men should pursue the Amalekites and that everything and everyone would be recovered.

Before going further, this is a matter that many struggle with in the records of the Old Testament. Why did God allow His chosen people to destroy other nations? Hadn't the other nations been occupying the land first to begin with? The Lord is holy. He is good. He is love. But this sure doesn't seem right in our minds.

Part of the answer is found in the book of Deuteronomy.

> *It is not by your righteousness or the uprightness of*
> *your heart that you are going in to possess their land.*
> *Rather, because of the wickedness of these nations,*
> *ADONAI your God is driving them out from before*
> *you, and in order to keep the word ADONAI swore*
> *to your fathers—to Abraham, to Isaac, and to Jacob.*
> *—Deuteronomy 9:5*

All the other nations had turned from the Lord. God cannot lie; thus, He will keep all His promises. Therefore, He chose the Israelites to show, as a Father, His goodness to. He saved them, undeservedly, out of many hardships. He spoke to them and gave them instructions on how to live good, pleasing, and holy lives. His relationship with them was intended to turn others to Him as they saw the protection and blessings upon His people. He did not limit His favor to the Israelites but accepted others who chose to come and live likewise. Let's read on about living under the Lord's favor.

Seeking out the Amalekites, David's men found an Egyptian in an open field and brought him to David, who fed and refreshed him. He was a slave of the Amalekites and had been abandoned in the field three days earlier because he was sick. In exchange for sparing his life and for not returning him to his master, the slave agreed to expose the location of the Amalekites. So, he led David and his men directly to them and they were found feasting and dancing over their victory and spoil. They attacked the marauders from twilight until evening the next day (1 Samuel 30:17), successfully recovered all that had been taken, and returned to Ziklag.

What can be learned from this celebratory revelry of "eating, drinking and feasting," or dancing? It did not result out of praise for God's goodness and faithfulness, but rather prideful boasting in self and man.

"Pride goes before destruction and a haughty
spirit before a fall."
—Proverbs 16:18

The lifestyles of generations past can be shocking to us. Imagine living in David's time when it was commonplace to raid and kill for daily sustenance. Everyone would need to be on guard constantly, always in fear of someone taking their food. When it seems everyone is against us, our response in times of trouble should be the same as David's. He sought God.

As children of God, we have special favor and protection. Certainly this does not mean we have favor to raid our neighbors! But in our distress, we can know that God desires that we first seek Him, and He will guide us through to victory.

In all your ways acknowledge Him and
He will make your paths straight.
—Proverbs 3:6

$$- 7 -$$

The Dance of David

*Meanwhile, David was dancing before ADONAI with
all his might while he was wearing a linen ephod.*
—2 Samuel 6:14

Oh, the famous dance of David. As with so many biblical events, this event is surrounded by controversy as well. With diligent study and insight, however, you'll realize this is truly a beautiful event clouded in human misunderstanding, hurting hearts, and glory and honor to God.

David's dance of exultant praise to God revolves around the Ark of the Covenant. God gave Moses specific instructions for building the Ark in Exodus 25. Inside the Ark, kept in the Holy of Holies—the most inner and most sacred room of the Tabernacle— was the Testimony that God gave Moses.

The Ark was to be a meeting place of God's holy presence and revelation where He would speak with Moses. The requirements for entering God's presence in the Holy Place within the Tent of Meeting were strict (Leviticus 16), as were the requirements for moving the Ark to future locations (Numbers 4). Failure to fulfill the exact requirements would lead to death.

The Lord was not happy with Israel's priests, Eli and his sons. His sons are described in 1 Samuel 2:12 as "worthless men" because they lived reckless and sinful lives and did not acknowledge the Lord. Samuel was being raised up and trained under Eli, to be a priest. The Lord favored him and spoke to him about the end of Eli and his sons because of their iniquity and refusal to change.

We find in 1 Samuel 4 that the Israelites went to battle against the Philistines and lost. Questioning why God allowed defeat in this battle, the Israelites decided to bring the Ark of the Covenant from its proper place in Shiloh, into their army's base camp at Ebenezer. They assumed that having the Ark in their presence would secure God's favor and their victory. The army gave such a great shout when the Ark was brought in that the Philistines heard it and were afraid. They thought there was no way they would win the next battle for they had heard of the great things God had done for the Israelites in Egypt.

The Philistines, however, mightily bolstered themselves to fight, and they triumphed over God's people. As the Israelites were defeated and fled, 30,000 of their soldiers died, and the Philistines captured the Ark. Two of Eli's sons died in the battle, and upon hearing the news, Eli fell, broke his neck, and also died.

The Philistines found that they were not faring well with the Ark of God in their possession. Many strange things occurred. The statue of their god, Dagon, toppled and broke before the Ark, tumors broke out on the people, and panic spread throughout the area. So, they decided to send the Ark back to its rightful place, along with guilt offerings of golden tumors and gold mice, intended to give glory to the God of Israel.

They loaded the Ark on a cart hitched to two milk cows and sent it to Beth-shemesh in the territory of the Israelites. There, Levites took the Ark from the cart and made offerings to the Lord. Naturally, curiosity got the better of some, and they decided to look inside the Ark. Remember, this is a sacred, holy instrument of the Lord's presence. The Lord struck down seventy men who had looked inside.

The Ark was then moved to Kiriath-jearim, into the house of Abinadab. His son, Eleazar, was consecrated to guard the Ark, and it remained in Kiriath-jearim for twenty years.

Meanwhile, Samuel had been raised up and was ministering to the people at that time. He directed them to turn their hearts back to the Lord and serve only Him. King Saul and his sons had previously died in battle, and David was reigning over Israel.

With a new king in place, the Philistines decide to attack once more. David sought God's advice about going up against the Philistines. The Lord told him to go, for he would have victory. David then set out with 30,000 chosen men to bring back the Ark of God from Abinadab's house. The Ark was placed on a new cart driven by two of Abinadab's sons.

As they traveled, David and all Israel with him were celebrating before the Lord with instruments of many kinds. Along the way, the oxen stumbled. Abinadab's son, Uzzah, reached out to steady the Ark, and when he grasped it, the Lord struck him down because of his irreverence. Frightened, angry, and grieved, King David left the Ark at the house of Obed-edom while he tried to figure out how to get the Ark home.

Three months later, David sought to bring back the Ark again. This time, instead of placing it on a cart led by cattle, David had carriers, or bearers, for the Ark and was prepared with sacrifices as the Lord required (see Exodus 25:14, Leviticus 1–8, and

1 Chronicles 15). God blessed this move since the Ark was being carried as God had established in His Word. So, He was pleased with the sacrifices and praise.

> *So David and the entire house of Israel brought up the*
> *ark of ADONAI with shouting and*
> *with the sound of the shofar.*
> *—2 Samuel 6:15*

What joy. What a celebration of victory. What honor to the Lord. He delights in His people. He desires that we wholeheartedly seek Him; hear His voice; trust Him completely; and act with wisdom, knowledge, and obedience. He is holy. He is good, and He will bless the ones who serve Him with all their heart, soul, and mind.

But the story is not over yet. What about David's first wife, Michal, King Saul's daughter? Didn't she see the dancing with her own eyes as they came into the city? Michal accused David of uncovering himself in front of the slave girls, "just as any vulgar fellow would shamelessly do" (2 Samuel 6:20).

Who are we to believe? Should we believe that David's dance pleased the Lord, or should we believe that Michal is correct in that David's behavior, his dance, was incredulously inappropriate? Read the next chapter for the answers to these questions.

$$- 8 -$$

David's Dance Despised

*But as the ark of ADONAI entered the city of David,
Saul's daughter Michal looked out of the window and
saw King David leaping and dancing before ADONAI,
so she despised him in her heart.*
—2 Samuel 6:16

*As the Ark of the Covenant of ADONAI came to the
City of David, Michal, Saul's daughter, looked out the
window. When she saw King David dancing and celebrating, she despised him in her heart.*
—1 Chronicles 15:29

This does not sound good—Michal despised David in her heart. Let's go back just a little ways to take in the whole picture and gain a better perspective. In Part One, Chapter 5: Victory Dances, we learned how David came to serve King Saul and that the king loved him. However, as David became more prominent, gaining attention from his valiant actions, Saul began to see him as a threat and sought ways to take David's life.

King Saul originally offered his eldest daughter, Merab, to David for marriage. However, before the time for marriage came,

Saul gave her to Adriel instead (1 Samuel 18:19). The next verse reveals that another daughter, Michal, loved David. Saul saw a deceptive opportunity and gave Michal to David in marriage because she would be a snare to him (verse twenty-one). How so? Would she be a convenient distraction to take David off his "game?" Could it be that Saul set the bridal dowry—100 Philistine foreskins—so high that he didn't think David would survive the challenge, let alone fully achieve it? He did achieve this goal and Michal became his wife.

No matter what Saul did, David continued in success. Moved by an evil spirit, Saul devised an assassination attempt. He threw a spear at David, hoping to pin him to the wall, but David fled and escaped. Saul then sent agents to watch David's house with the order to kill him in the morning, but Michal warned him and helped him escape. Rather than cooperating with her father, she lied to Saul's messengers to distract them while David fled (1 Samuel 19:13–17). Saul sought David's life even more aggressively, preventing him from returning to Michal.

David was on the run from King Saul and living in the wilderness. During this time he took two more wives; Abigail and Ahinoam (1 Samuel 25:39, 43). We also find out what happened to Michal.

> *Meanwhile Saul had given Michal his daughter, David's*
> *wife, to Palti son of Laish, who was of Gallim.*
> *—1 Samuel 25:44*

Let's fast-forward to 2 Samuel, following Saul's death, a few more wives and children for David, and his victory over the house of Saul. Saul's uncle and army commander, Abner, betrayed the house of Saul after being confronted over sleeping with one of Saul's concubines (2 Samuel 3:7–10). So here is a man who was no longer for the house of Saul, but he might be of use to David. David agreed to cut a covenant with Abner, and this is what we learn:

> *"Good!" said David. "I will cut a covenant with you. But one thing I require of you: you will not see my face unless you first bring Saul's daughter Michal when you come to see my face." Then David sent messengers to Saul's son Ish-bosheth demanding, "Give me my wife Michal, whom I betrothed to myself for 100 Philistine foreskins." So Ish-bosheth sent and took her from her husband, Paltiel son of Laish. But her husband accompanied her, weeping as he went, and followed her as far as Bahurim. Then Abner said to him, "Go, return!" So he returned.*
> *—2 Samuel 3:13–16*

It would seem that Paltiel—from the tribe of Benjamin—loved and adored Michal. What had happened in Michal's heart during this time? What had her father told her about David—from the tribe of Judah—when he fled? Did she forget her love for David as Paltiel stayed close by, loved and provided for her? Did she become too comfortable as a doted-upon wife? Was she over the stress and turmoil of being married to David, a man of war who fled for his life from her father's jealousy and hatred? She was then torn from Paltiel and forced by her brother Ish-bosheth to return to David, but we soon find out her heart toward him had changed.

Following Saul's death, David continued working to establish his kingdom according to the will of the Lord. This included bringing back the Ark of the Covenant, which the Philistines had stolen in battle. The first attempt to recover it had failed miserably.

So, David sought the Lord and His ways to bring back this holy and sacred Ark in the manner the Lord had prescribed instead of the quick and easy way of man. When the Lord blessed the second attempt, after six careful and holy steps, David provided sacrifices and broke out in dance to the Lord.

The dancing and sacrificial offerings continued as the Ark was brought into the city to its resting place in a tent that David had set up for it. Michal, who was likely bitter in heart over her forced return to David, watched the whole joyful scene from a window.

Unaware of Michal's observance and her conflicted heart, David was filled with joy, thankfulness, and a celebratory spirit because of the Lord's blessing. David blessed the people in the name of the Lord and distributed a multitude of food gifts before returning home "to bless his own household" (2 Samuel 6:20a).

At this point Michal ungratefully confronts David, accusing him of inappropriate, shameless behavior. Imagine his shock at this shift in the atmosphere.

> *But Saul's daughter Michal came out to meet David and*
> *said, "How the king of Israel distinguished himself*
> *today, when he uncovered himself today in the eyes of*
> *the slave girls of his subjects, as any vulgar fellow*
> *would shamelessly uncover himself!"*
> *—2 Samuel 6:20b*

*"It was before ADONAI," David said to Michal, "who
chose me instead of your father and all his household,
appointing me ruler over the people of ADONAI, over
Israel! So I danced before ADONAI, and will dishonor
myself even more than this, and will be low in my own
eyes. Yet in the eyes of the slave girls whom you
mentioned, I will be honored."*
—2 Samuel 6:21–22

*So Saul's daughter Michal had no children
to the day of her death.*
—2 Samuel 6:23

Here it's important to cover a couple of possible misinterpretations. God is not a God of confusion, and every word in the Bible is true. So when something that seems contradictory creeps up, it is our understanding that is lacking, not the Word of God. Sadly, many will teach from the lack rather than search out the matter.

The first issue is Michal's accusation that David "uncovered himself." There are pictures circulating in the world—even in some Bible illustrations—of David removing his clothing and dancing in a loin cloth. This has led to a lot of perplexity regarding David's behavior. Here is what the scripture says.

*Meanwhile, David was dancing before ADONAI with
all his might while he was wearing a linen ephod.*
—2 Samuel 6:14

An ephod is the outer garment that all the Hebrew priests wore. Was Michal accusing with exaggerated sarcasm because

David was not wearing his kingly robes, and in her resentful attitude she found this offensive? More specific details are available in 1 Chronicles 15, which relays the same event. After a disastrous first attempt, moving and restoring the Ark was not to be taken lightly a second time. This corresponding scripture tells us about the sacred preparation that took place. It will benefit you greatly if you take the time to read the entire chapter, but here is a snippet for you.

> *Now David was clothed with a robe of fine linen, as were*
> *all the Levites who were carrying the Ark, and as were*
> *the singers and Henaniah the leader of the songs of the*
> *singers. David also wore a linen ephod.*
> *—1 Chronicles 15:27*

Did David remove the robe and tie up the ephod to move more freely? There is no mention of that. The Word simply indicates he was indeed dressed appropriately.

A second point of controversy is connected with 2 Samuel 6:23, which states that Michal had no children. In 2 Samuel 21:8, the verse seemingly contradicts, saying that she had five sons.

> *But the king took the two sons of Rizpah daughter of*
> *Aiah, whom she bore to Saul—Armoni and Mephibo-*
> *sheth; also the five sons of Michal daughter of*
> *Saul, whom she bore to Adriel son of*
> *Barzillai the Meholathite…*
> *—2 Samuel 21:8*

We know from 1 Samuel 18:19 that Michal's sister, Merab, was married to Adriel. Some Bible versions list the sons as Merab's, and others list them as Michal's. Which is correct? To learn the truth of this verse, we must dig deeper. Let's compare a few commonly used Bible versions.

TLV	*...also the five sons of Michal daughter of Saul, whom she bore to Adriel son of Barzillai the Meholathite.*
KJV	*...and the five sons of Michal the daughter of Saul, whom she brought up for Adriel the son of Barzillai the Meholathite.*
NIV	*...together with the five sons of Saul's daughter Merab, whom she had borne to Adriel son of Barzillai the Meholathite*
NLT	*He also gave them the five sons of Saul's daughter Merab, the wife of Adriel son of Barzillai from Meholah.*

John Gill's *Exposition of the Bible Commentary* (*biblestudytools.com*) provides an explanation based on the wording of the King James Version. It states that the phrase *brought up,* is a Targum, signifying that she *bore* them. Merriam-Webster.com defines "Targum" as an Aramaic translation or paraphrase of a portion of the Old Testament. This indicates the original phrase was difficult to translate into English. Knowing what we do about Merab and Michal, it seems logical to surmise that something must have happened to Merab, and Michal was the woman who raised her children.

When considering all of God's Word, there appears to be no contradiction. God does not contradict. He is holy. He is trustworthy. He is above all other gods. He is worthy of all praise. As you read these stories in context and in their entirety, God always reveals Himself as a God of mercy, our God of redemption, our God of love.

What are we to learn of Michal's response? Was she justified in her frustration, her anger, her attack? If you had been in her situation, would you have responded differently? We have the benefit of hindsight, but likely, we have at times responded to our own difficult circumstances in a similar way.

God's ways, however, are better. As we mature, we can trust God to redeem our circumstances and bring blessings from them—if we respond wisely. Give Him control in difficult situations. He does wondrous deeds for His beloved children who are submitted to and led by Him.

> *Blessed is one who is always cautious, but whoever*
> *hardens his heart will fall into trouble.*
> *—Proverbs 28:14*

> *Do not be quickly provoked in your spirit, for anger set-*
> *tles in the bosom of fools.*
> *—Ecclesiastes 7:9*

> *Set a guard, ADONAI, over my mouth. Keep watch*
> *over the door of my lips.*
> *—Psalm 141:3*

What do we now make of David's dancing? It was a glorious dance to the Lord, and God was pleased. David sought God's heart and God's regulations regarding the holy things. He did God's will regarding the Ark, to properly govern, bless the people, and the land. David's dance was a great rejoicing to the Lord, and He was pleased.

Rejoice in the Lord always—again I will say, rejoice!
—Philippians 4:4

– 9 –

Dancing Prophets of Baal

So they took the bull that he gave them, prepared it,
and called on the name of Baal from morning till
noon, crying, "O Baal, answer us!" But there
was no voice—no one was answering. They
also danced leaping around the
altar that was made.
—1 Kings 18:26

Moving on from David's reign, Israel had relative peace for forty years during the reign of his son, Solomon. Power is often a difficult thing to handle wisely. Even Solomon, the wisest person to ever live, compromised his ways and did not fully follow the Lord.

After Solomon, many kings, commanders, and priests rose and fell—each one seemingly worse than the previous. It was an unusual thing for Israel to have a king who continually did his best to reign according to God's Word and ways. Few had success, and what success they did experience was quickly taken away by the next power-hungry self-exalting ruler. It is truly a wonder that God puts up with humanity and keeps every word, promise, and covenant He has spoken.

Solomon's son, Rehoboam, took up the crown following Solomon's death. During Rehoboam's reign the kingdom was split in two. Rehoboam ruled the region of Judah, consisting of the tribes of Judah and Benjamin. Jeroboam (Solomon's servant, an Ephraimite) was king over Israel, which consisted of the other ten tribes.

Following Rehoboam, his son Abijam ruled Judah for three years, and then his son Asa became king. Asa was one of the few who did his best to follow in David's footsteps to do what was right according to the Lord. In the 38th year of Asa's reign, Ahab became king over Israel. Ahab followed in the footsteps of the increasingly wicked rulers before him (1 Kings 16:30).

God's prophet, Elijah, proclaimed to wicked Ahab that there would be no rain or even dew in the land. Often times, a prophet would be imprisoned or killed if they did not prophesy according to the king's desires, but Elijah was faithful to the Lord and declared to Ahab everything that the Lord spoke to him. God then directed Elijah to safe places where He miraculously provided for him during this time. In the third year of the famine, God told Elijah to meet with Ahab, and then the rains would come.

> *Now when Ahab saw Elijah, Ahab said to him, "Is it*
> *you, the one who causes trouble for Israel?"*
> —*1 Kings 18:17*

Can't you just sense the resentment and dishonor seething from Ahab's mouth in that verse? Elijah replies that it is Ahab and his family who had not followed the ways of the Lord and therefore had brought trouble on Israel. He then challenged Ahab to gather his prophets, the prophets of Baal and Asherah, and have them offer the sacrifice of a young bull to their god. Elijah would do the same, calling upon the name of his God. The one who answered by consuming the sacrifice with fire would be revealed as the true God of Israel.

Ahab agreed to the challenge. His prophets cried out to Baal, but there was no answer. They danced and leaped about, shouted even louder, and cut themselves with swords and spears—which was a custom in their culture—to incite a response from their god, but there was still no answer. They carried on for most of the day.

When evening came, Elijah called the people to him. He built an altar in the name of the Lord; filled the surrounding trench; and soaked the wood on the altar, as well as the bull offering that lied upon it, with water. He added even more water, and at the time of the evening sacrifice Elijah called out to the Lord.

> *Then the fire of ADONAI fell and consumed the burnt offering—and the wood, the stones and the dust—and licked up the water that was in the trench. When all the people saw it, they fell on their faces and they said, "ADONAI, He is God! ADONAI, He is God!"*
> *—1 Kings 18:38–39*

At Elijah's command, the prophets of Baal were captured and slaughtered. He then sent Ahab to "eat and drink," declaring to him that the rains were coming. Elijah and his servant climbed to the top of Carmel, and after praying seven times, a dark windy storm arose, releasing a flood of rain on the land.

When Ahab told his wife Jezebel what had taken place with Elijah, and that all the prophets had been slain, she sent messengers threatening to have Elijah killed. He fled in fear and hid until the Lord sent an angel to encourage and strengthen him. God revealed His power and might to Elijah through the wind and an earthquake, but He revealed His authority and presence through a soft whisper. Elijah was strengthened, and the Lord gave him specific instructions.

In time, Ahab and Jezebel die unpleasant deaths (1 Kings 22:37, 2 Kings 9:33). At the end of Elijah's earthly days, however, the Lord took him up in a chariot of fire in a whirlwind (2 Kings 2:1–12).

In our study of biblical dance thus far, there is a recognizable difference between the dance of those who serve other gods and the dance of God's people. Worldly dances are either self-serving or a means to invite a response from the demonic spiritual world, neither of which is pleasing to the Lord. In contrast, Miriam's dance, David's dance, and even the annual dances of Shiloh, were all offered in celebration and with joy in response to the good acts that God had already done. These dances bring honor and delight to the Lord.

Dancing Goat-demons

*But desert creatures will lie there. Their houses will be
full of owls. Ostriches will dwell there,
and goat-demons will dance there.*
—Isaiah 13:21

Now isn't this interesting? What in the world are goat-demons, and in what kind of place do they dance? The word *dance* in the TLV means to leap about. Other Bible versions use "frolic" and "caper."

Isaiah 13 is the beginning of an oracle, which is a burden, or a weighty message, regarding Babylon. Merriam-Webster.com describes Babylon as a city devoted to materialism and sensual pleasures. Symbolically, Babylon often refers to spiritually heathen nations. Isaiah saw into end-time events and wrote the vision down.

The chapter begins with the description of the Lord gathering and preparing His people for battle "to destroy the whole land." Elements in the heavens: the stars, the constellations, the sun, and the moon, will no longer give light. This specific event is also repeated in Matthew 24:29 and Revelation 8:12.

The rest of the chapter details horrific times. The destruction is so great in fact that it rivals the desolation of Sodom and Gomorrah, which is never to be inhabited again, except by desert creatures including owls, ostriches, goat-demons, hyenas, and jackals.

In Isaiah 14:1–11 Isaiah speaks of Israel's restoration in their own land. In Isaiah 14:12–21, we get a glimpse of how far the "Shining One"—a reference to Lucifer—fell from the heights of heaven and the presence of God's glory to deep darkness and the "lowest parts of the Pit," along with his children, the offspring of evildoers.

Back to our verse about dance. Maybe you're thinking, as I did, *I've seen owls and ostriches, and I know what hyenas and jackals are, but what is a goat-demon?* Good question. The King James Version describes these creatures as satyrs. Still no visual? Me neither. According to the *New Strong's Expanded Exhaustive Concordance of the Bible*, the original Hebrew word used is *Saiyr*, or *Sair* (saw-eer'). It is a noun that refers to a shaggy creature, possibly a he-goat.

By analogy, it also represents a faun, or a being that was an object of pagan worship, which Leviticus 17:7 and 2 Chronicles 11:15 translate as "devil" or "goat-idol." In Isaiah, goat-demons do not seem to be anything in demonic form, but rather a desolate place occupied only by various wilderness creatures. Maybe "wild goats" in the NIV is a better translation in this instance.

In Leviticus 16, God's instructions to the Levitical priests required that he-goats be used on the Day of Atonement: one for a sin offering, and the other for a scapegoat. The priest was to present the scapegoat before the Lord, place the sins of the people upon it, and then send it into the wilderness.

While Isaiah 13:21 is not referring to any form of human dance, this portion of God's Word clarifies that He is a holy God, and He will not tolerate the evil operating in the world, spewing from Babylon, forever. He will save the people He has called His own, one day evil will be completely annihilated… and we will dance!

– 11 –

Dances of Merrymakers

Again I will build you, so you will be rebuilt, virgin Israel! Again you will take up your tambourines as ornaments, and go out to dances of merrymakers.
—Jeremiah 31:4

Then will the virgin rejoice in the dance, both young men and old men together. For I will turn their mourning into joy, and I will comfort them, and make them rejoice out of their sorrow.
—Jeremiah 31:13

If you have ever wondered what God's attitude is about dancing, these two verses are for you. What great joy the Lord has over His children merrily dancing, praising, worshiping, and rejoicing in Him and His goodness, especially when it is in response to what He does, has done, and will do.

The verses above are part of a word from the Lord to Jeremiah regarding Israel's future following their seventy-year exile in Babylon. God had been warning them to obey Him or He would uproot them. It seemed that no one would listen to what the Lord was saying through His prophet, Jeremiah: not the priests, the other prophets, or the people. What a difficult job Jeremiah had to repeatedly warn a people who refused to listen. He must have experienced times of great doubt about whether he was hearing God clearly. But the Lord promised Jeremiah that He was with him and had appointed him as His prophet to declare His Word.

> *"Before I formed you in the womb, I knew you,*
> *and before you were born, I set you apart—*
> *I appointed you prophet to the nations."*
> *—Jeremiah 1:5*
>
> *"Though they will fight against you, they will not win,*
> *for I am with you, to deliver you."*
> *It is a declaration of ADONAI.*
> *—Jeremiah 1:19*

These two verses show it is God who creates and appoints our positions in life. He speaks to us, and as we choose to obey what He says, He is with us and for us. Jeremiah faithfully spoke God's Word to His people, often in tears because of his lonely position, and grief over the people's disbelief. Off into Babylonian exile the people went for their continued disobedience to the Lord.

Yet God always loves, always redeems, always gives hope, and always restores. He promised good things would follow this time of discipline if His people would return their hearts and minds to Him.

For I know the plans that I have in mind for you,"
declares ADONAI, "plans for shalom and not
calamity—to give you a future and a hope.
Then you will call on Me and come and pray to Me, and
I will listen to you. You will seek Me and find Me, when
you will search for Me with all your heart. Then I will
be found by you," says ADONAI, "and I will return
you from exile and gather you from all the nations and
from all the places where I have driven you," says ADO-
NAI, "and I will bring you back to the place from which
I removed you as captives into exile."
—Jeremiah 29:11–14

Jeremiah 29–31 is the Word of the Lord declaring that after a time of disciplining the Israelites, He will bring them back into the land He gave them. His love for His people is so deep and so strong. These chapters are rich in exposing His swift and stern discipline, the goal being to restore and protect His loved ones. He does the same for us today. As followers of Christ, we need to understand how the Lord wants us to follow Him. He will discipline us for a time, but that is for our benefit. Let's look at the main chapter verses again, but this time, let's also examine the preceding verse to each.

"From afar ADONAI appeared to me." "Yes, I have
loved you with an everlasting love. Therefore I have
drawn you with lovingkindness. Again I will build you,
so you will be rebuilt, virgin Israel! Again you will
take up your tambourines as ornaments, and go
out to dances of merrymakers."
—Jeremiah 31:3–4

They will come and sing on Zion's height, radiant over
the bounty of ADONAI—over the grain, the wine, the
oil, and the young of the flock. Their life will be like a
watered garden, and they will never languish again.
Then will the virgin rejoice in the dance, both young
men and old men together. For I will turn their
mourning into joy, and I will comfort them,
and make them rejoice out of their sorrow.
—Jeremiah 31:12–13

What beautiful, hope-filled, inspiring words from our Lord God about the future of Israel. He speaks not only of Israel's return after the exile, but also of a future time—the new covenant, hinting toward the millennial reign of Christ and eternity.

"…It will never be uprooted or thrown
down again—forever."
—Jeremiah 31:40b

The Lord Himself describes His children as going out with tambourines as ornaments to dances of merrymakers. They are joyful, shouting, praising, their mourning is turned into joy, and they understand and are satisfied with His goodness. Oh yes, God approves of dancing: then, now, and especially in the future.

Read those verses again. Dwell on them. God's Word isn't just for the Israelites. If you are a born-again follower of the Lord Jesus Christ, you are indeed grafted in and have all the benefits that apply to the children of Israel. He desires everyone to be close to Him.

*...know then that those who have faith are children of
Abraham. The Scriptures, foreseeing that God would
justify the Gentiles by faith, proclaimed the Good News
to Abraham in advance, saying, "All the nations shall be
blessed through you." So then, the faithful are blessed
along with Abraham, the faithful one.*
—*Galatians 3:7–9*

Our fullness of life is found in God. Have you ever experienced
a separation from the comfortable things of this life, and what may
feel like a separation from His presence? Separations such as this
exile and such as those you may have experienced are meant to
cause us to see our shortcomings and return to the Lord.

*There is neither Jew nor Greek, there is neither slave nor
free, there is neither male nor female—for you are all
one in Messiah Yeshua. And if you belong to Messiah,
then you are Abraham's seed—heirs
according to the promise.*
—*Galatians 3:28–29*

Oh, I tell you! He loves you so much. You are accepted. You are
included as a recipient of His promises: peace; a future; hope; a return to your land; destruction of your enemies; freedom from
former bondages; quiet and ease; healing; thanksgiving and the
sound of celebration; joy; everlasting love; and, best of all, the light
of His continual presence. We can freely dance in praise and worship to our God. He rebuilds and restores. We rejoice.

$$- 12 -$$

God's Dance of Joy

ADONAI your God is in your midst—a mighty Savior!
He will delight over you with joy. He will quiet you
with His love. He will dance for joy over you
with singing.
—Zephaniah 3:17

The Lord's great love toward us overwhelms and fills me with awe and wonder. What does the word *joy* mean to you? What comes to your mind's eye when you hear that word? Do you believe He loves you so much that He will actually dance for joy over you?

As a mother, I remember dancing with each of my babies. I rocked and gently danced with them to comfort and calm them. I danced with them to express love and joy and for pleasure and fun. They were my precious children, and I wanted them close so they would know they were loved, and that I enjoyed being with them. How much more so does the Lord do the same?

Zephaniah is a powerful book consisting of three prophetic chapters, written during the time of King Josiah's reign. Following a long period of wicked kings, Josiah did much good to restore the people to God. Despite his positive leadership and the reestablishment of worship to God, upon his death, society quickly returned to its evil ways.

The prophecy of Zephaniah is very Revelation-like as it describes the day of ADONAI (Zephaniah 1:7), also refered to as the day of ADONAI's anger (Zephaniah 2:2), and the day of ADONAI's wrath (Zephaniah 2:3). This day signifies the time that God will bring an end to evil and those who practice it. For His people who chose to follow and worship Him, rather than destruction, they will experience restoration; a time of salvation, peace and joy in the tangible presence of the Lord (Zephaniah 3:9-20).

Chapter one describes the day of ADONAI, which will be the total annihilation of man and beast from the face of the earth.

Neither their silver nor their gold will be able to rescue
them on the day of ADONAI's wrath. With the fire of
His passion the entire earth will be consumed.
—Zephaniah 1:18

Because God's people sinned and turned away from Him, God's wrath will be poured out upon the earth in such a great measure that nothing and no one will survive. Even the earth will ultimately be destroyed. We know from Revelation 21 that there will be a new heaven and a new earth, so chapter one could likely reference the old earth being completely destroyed before God brings forth the New Jerusalem and the new heaven and earth.

Chapter two gives just a bit of hope for a few, calling God's remnant to repent and seek Him before this terrible day arrives so that they might be hidden from it. The surrounding nations of Israel will be destroyed and the coast given to Judah.

The word of ADONAI is against you, Canaan, the land
of the Philistines, and I will destroy you until there is no
inhabitant. The seacoast will become pastures, with
meadows for shepherds and folds for flocks. The coast
will belong to the remnant of the house of Judah, upon
which they will graze. In the houses of Ashkelon they
will lie down in the evening. For ADONAI their God
will visit them and return them from captivity.
—Zephaniah 2:5b–7

God will devastate all the people, cities and nations that have mistreated His people. These are Gaza; Ashkelon; Ashdod; Ekron; the Cherethites; and Canaan, the land of the Philistines. These verses describe a complete change of the land. The cities mentioned are along the seacoast and are still there today (Ekron may refer to the mound of Tel Migne, or Khirbet el-Muqanna in Arabic, about 22 miles west of Jerusalem).

Also, God's people will live in the houses of those who were destroyed. Chapter one mentions that the wicked nations who build houses will not live in them (verse thirteen). Chapter two speaks of the land being plundered by God's remnant (verse nine). Zephaniah also prophesies an end, or a wasting away of all the gods of the earth. In this chapter, destruction and removal of all that is wicked continues, followed by salvation and hope for a repentant, believing remnant.

Chapters one and two of Zephaniah are pretty shocking, and it is easy to want to pass quickly through them and not return. However, I hope you will see how God faithfully reveals His plans to warn, guide, protect, and save His people. These verses, spoken of a future time through Zephaniah, are an indication that God is certainly long-suffering, patient with humanity, not wanting any of His creation to perish. However, He is a holy and just God and will not continue forever with those who mistreat others, choosing to do evil. They have been warned.

As a loving Father, God will chastise us, rebuke us, correct us, and restore us. He loved Judah and wanted them to choose Him and His ways, which would be a blessing to them. Humanity is no different today. We choose to go our own way. We are double-minded; we believe we are right with God, but we do not give Him much time or say in our lives. Then we wonder why things don't work out well for us.

Chapter three continues with God revealing the coming destruction of Jerusalem. The first half speaks of God's people, who did not obey, trust, or seek Him. As a result, their cities will be laid waste, and again, the fire of God's wrath will consume all the earth (verse eight). God then reminds us there is a faithful remnant. God always has a remnant. Israel, and all of God's children, will be restored.

The second half of chapter three speaks of complete restoration. Having cleansed the earth, God restores His people, removing the proud and arrogant, leaving the meek and humble in a beautiful and safe place where the Lord is in their midst. Life described in this portion of scripture sounds wonderful: pure speech, no shame, no lies, singing, rejoicing and exulting, no fear, and God's presence. He will do away with all evil and wickedness, and we will know absolutely how much He delights in us. We can get close to knowing that by studying His Word and fully committing our lives to Him now. Let's choose to be part of His remnant that will be hidden and spared.

Take a look again at this chapter's headline scripture, Zephaniah 3:17. The word translated as *dance* is *gîyl* (gheel) or *gûwl* (gool) in Hebrew. It means to spin round (under the influence of any violent emotion) or to rejoice (be glad, joy, be joyful, rejoice). Other versions interpret this word as joy or rejoice.

Below is the King James Version, which translates the verse a little differently.

> *The Lord thy God in the midst of thee is mighty; he will*
> *save, he will rejoice over thee with joy; he will rest in his*
> *love, he will joy over thee with singing.*
> *—Zephaniah 3:17, KJV*

Looking at the KJV phrase, "rejoice over thee with joy," the Hebrew word for *rejoice* is *sûws* (soos); or *sîys*, (sece). It means to be bright or cheerful (greatly be glad, joy, make mirth, rejoice). Then there is the word *joy*. This is the word *simchâh* (sim-khaw'), which means blithesomeness or glee, how one might act at a religious gathering or festival (exceeding or fullness of gladness, joy, mirth, pleasure, rejoicing).

The second *joy*—"he will joy over thee with singing"—is from the Hebrew word *gîyl* (gheel) or *gûwl* (gool), which I have already described. As dancers, do we not at times spin round as we listen to or sing praise or worship songs? Can you see where we get that from—from the Lord, Himself? He is the creator of dancing or spinning with great emotion. Since we are made in His image, we can respond to Him in the same manner.

Each interpretation or translation holds truth, and our understanding is enhanced through studying the original language to prevent confusion. The bottom line is that because of His great emotion for you, the Lord is actively engaged in expressing His heart and thoughts toward you. I like the dance interpretation; don't you? Can you imagine that coming time when evil is completely gone and we are forever with the Lord without any hindrance? We will be dancing with Him, full of great emotion and love.

– 13 –

Restoration Dance

You turned my mourning into dancing. You removed
my sackcloth and clothed me with joy.
—Psalm 30:12

Our God, Elohim, is the Creator of all things: of heaven and earth
and everything in them. Included in "everything" is mankind—
each individual with unique gifts and talents, established at specific times and places—to work together with Him in His goodness
so that all people have the opportunity to be drawn to Him. Nothing is of our own doing; everything we do comes from Him. David
knew this in the depths of his being, and he lived to seek, know,
and honor God. The first verse of Psalm 30 gives us its purpose
and authorship.

A psalm, a song for the dedication of the Temple, of David.
—Psalm 30:1

The word *Temple* is translated in other Bible versions as *house*.
The original Hebrew word is *Bayith*. It has a multitude of meanings
including house, household, permanent dwelling place, a place of
worship or sanctuary, rooms or wings of a house, receptacle, royal
court, territory, or country.

While the TLV Bible capitalizes "Temple," which indicates its great importance, other versions do not. A comma after "Temple," followed by "of David" indicates the psalm is of—or was written by—David. Other versions omit the comma, making it sound like the temple or house was David's personal residence. Scholars are divided as to whether the song was written for the dedication of David's home, or for the dedication of the Temple that would be built by his son, Solomon. Even when we read the words of the Psalm, it is difficult to distinguish its purpose.

Elsewhere in the Bible, we find David's home briefly mentioned.

Then King Hiram of Tyre sent envoys to David with
cedar logs, carpenters and masons; and they
build a palace for David.
—2 Samuel 5:11

So David lived in a grand palace as he reigned, but the Ark of the Covenant, the place of God's presence, remained "within curtains," that is, in the Tent of Meeting. As a blessing to God, David desired to build a house for the Ark, but the Lord had other plans. This incredible dialogue between David, Nathan the prophet, and the Lord, found in 2 Samuel 7, gives us a glimpse of the greatness of God as He refers to David's seed, who will build a house for His name. It also refers to a house that God would build for His servant, hinting at the future time and reign of Jesus. I encourage you to take a few minutes now to read 2 Samuel 7 in your Bible, which describes the Lord's promise to David. Even before the birth of Christ, the angel Gabriel spoke to Mary about this eternal throne for all humanity, established by the Lord (Luke 1:32–33).

Through the prophet, Nathan, God revealed His promises and plans for Israel's future and blessed David by saying his son, Solomon, would be the one to build His house (2 Samuel 7:14, 1 Chronicles 28:6). Full of gratitude toward the Lord, David commissioned Solomon to build the Temple he had desired to build for God.

A record of all the donations David made to the Temple, as well as praises, blessings, and sacrifices, are listed in 1 Chronicles 29. Included was much gold, silver, copper, iron, and wood; every kind of precious stone and abundant marble; as well as David's private treasure of gold and silver. Other leaders also willingly contributed gold, silver, bronze, iron, and precious stones. The people rejoiced and gave willingly. Their attitude is revealed in David's words:

> *"But who am I and who are my people that we should be*
> *able to offer so willingly as this? For everything*
> *comes from You, and from Your hand*
> *we have given to You."*
> *—1 Chronicles 29:14*

> *"…With integrity of heart I have willingly offered all*
> *these things. And now I have seen with joy Your*
> *people who are present here willingly*
> *contribute to You."*
> *—1 Chronicles 29:17*

After completion of the Temple, Solomon led its dedication, which included fourteen days of feasting (see 1 Kings 8).

Throughout this thirteen-verse Psalm, David praises God for bringing him through his many trials and for protecting him from his enemies. He contrasts the grief of experiencing the Lord's discipline with the joy of restoration. In God's goodness and graciousness, David's mourning is turned into dancing, and he declares he will praise the Lord forever.

Whether Psalm 30 was written for the dedication of David's personal palace or for the dedication of the Temple for the Ark, it is clear that the whole Psalm glorifies God for His blessings and His leading of David's life. While the Psalm is personal to David, we can also make it personal to our own lives in our worship of the Lord. God is gracious. God is good. He delivers and restores us to dancing, joy, and fullness of life.

$$- 14 -$$

Fountains of Joy

Then singing and dancing—all my
fountains of joy are in you!
—Psalm 87:7

Psalm 87 is a song written in seven joyful verses. Not every Bible version includes the word *dancing*. The table below compares a few other popular versions.

TLV	*Then singing and dancing—all my fountains of joy are in you!*
NKJV	*Both the singers and the players on instruments say, "All my springs are in you."*
NIV	*As they make music they will sing, "All my fountains are in you."*
NASB	*Then those who sing as well as those who play the flutes shall say, "All my springs of joy are in you."*

In comparing these four versions, we see that the TLV is the only one that mentions dancing. Does that mean that either the

TLV or the other versions misinterpreted the verse? It can be difficult to go back in history and know exactly what an author meant and then translate that meaning into present-day language.

Using a concordance based on an Old English translation can leave one (i.e., me) a bit frustrated in doing research, so let's look at one more version. The Complete Jewish Bible (CJB) interprets the verse this way:

> Singers and dancers alike say, "For me, you are the
> source of everything."
> —Psalm 87:7, CJB

Many commentators have tried to explain verse seven, but each has a different opinion about what the verse means. So, I will add my own opinion. Considering those who interpreted the TLV and CJB were likely more familiar with the Hebrew language than, say, the interpreters of the King James Version, I will go with the versions that mention "dancing" and "dancers." Realize, however, that as a worship dancer, I may be a bit partial, but in my mind's eye, even the phrase "springs of joy" connotes visions of leaping, spinning, and dancing rather than flowing water.

Quiet your own heart and mind for a moment and read the whole Psalm for yourself. Keep in mind that this is a joyful song and that the Lord is pleased when you read His Word.

Psalm 87

¹ A psalm of the sons of Korah, a song.
His foundation is in the holy mountains.

² ADONAI loves the gates of Zion more
than all the dwellings of Jacob.
³ Glorious things are spoken of you,
city of God. Selah

⁴ "I will mention Rahab and Babylon
among those who acknowledge Me—
behold Philistia and Tyre, with Cush:
'This one was born there.'"

⁵ But of Zion it will be said:
"This one and that one were born in her."
And Elyon Himself will establish her.

⁶ ADONAI will count in the register of the peoples:
"This one was born there." Selah
⁷ Then singing and dancing—
all my fountains of joy are in you!

This Psalm can be challenging to comprehend as the translation is difficult, and for many of us, the historical significance is unfamiliar. Let's look at it verse by verse. The word *foundation* in verse one figuratively represents a "beginning." We can tell from the verses that follow that "holy mountains" likely refers to Jerusalem.

"Zion" in verse two is a word that represents the Davidic monarchy, and literally means "marked" or "distinctive."

What is the "city of God" in verse three? David was born in Bethlehem (1 Samuel 17:12). When he became king, in battle against the Jebusites, he took the citadel—or stronghold—of Zion, which was within Jerusalem (2 Samuel 5:7). It became known as the city of David once he took up his reign there.

Our Lord and Savior was also born in Bethlehem, He gave up His life for us at Golgotha in Jerusalem, and He will yet reign in the new Jerusalem, thus giving us insight that the city of David is also the city of God (Psalm 87:3).

Elsewhere in the Bible, Zechariah gives us a little more understanding of the three locations mentioned in the first three verses: holy mountains, Zion, and city of God.

> *"Thus says ADONAI-Tzva'ot, "I am exceedingly zealous for Zion, I am burning with jealousy for her." Thus says ADONAI, "I will return to Zion and dwell in the midst of Jerusalem. Then Jerusalem will be called the City of Truth and the mountain of ADONAI-Tzva'ot will be called the Holy Mountain."*
> *—Zechariah 8:2-3*

In Zechariah 8:2, the Lord of Hosts is exceedingly zealous and burning with jealousy for Zion, reflecting His love for Zion which is mentioned in Psalm 87:2. Simply put, Zion is synonymous with Jerusalem, God's holy mountain, and the city of God.

Psalm 48:2-3 also confirm these special places. While descriptions of these locations may not be as familiar to us today, they were common-place knowledge during David's time.

"Rahab and Babylon" (verse four) are symbolic of Egypt, Philistia and Tyre—regions along the coast of Israel—and Cush, the region south of Egypt. We learn from the book of Ezekiel that God pronounced vengeance and judgments on several coastal cities because in their pride, they had scorned Israel in her destruction. The

Lord will restore Israel, and the people from these costal regions surrounding Zion will acknowledge the one born in the city of God, that is, David. Or is this verse possibly a symbolic reference to Christ? Both possibilities are referenced by scholars and commentators.

Verses five and six give us a look into the future that those born in Zion *will* be spoken of; Elyon (the Most High) *will* establish the city; and ADONAI has a register or written record from which He *will* count the one that was born there.

The Psalm concludes with singing and dancing in verse seven; images of fountains or springs of joy; and expressions of love, rejoicing, and delight. With some understanding, this Psalm becomes a beautiful declaration of God's majesty and His love for this city and its people.

– 15 –

Praise Dancing

*Let them praise His Name with dancing. Let them sing
praises to Him with tambourine and harp.*
—*Psalm 149:3*

*Praise Him with tambourine and dance. Praise Him
with string instruments and flute.*
—*Psalm 150:4*

These two verses from the Psalms mentioning dance as a form of praise are two of the most commonly known among those who dance for the Lord. Why are they so important? They definitively declare dance as an acceptable form of praise to God.

Over the years, many churches have turned away from and shut their doors on dancing. Some emphatically exclude dance because of its provocative or sinful nature. As we have learned so far from studying the Word, dance in and of itself is not sinful. Remember, all things were created by God. However, we have an enemy that has enticed humanity to turn dance into something personal, something that focuses on humanity's fleshly selfishness, in order to divert us from its goodness. Our enemy's goal is to steal, kill, and destroy anything and everything that originates from God because everything that comes from God is good. He subtly deceives and lies until we believe the lies, which, in this case, is the lie that dancing is evil and that a Christ-follower must avoid it.

What is God's perspective? Dance is a form of praise and rejoicing that we can offer back to Him in response to His great love, goodness, and mercy toward us.

Are you still not convinced?

Reread Dances of Merrymakers. It is the Lord that rebuilds and tells Israel to take up tambourines as ornaments and go out to dances.

Reread Dances of Shiloh. Those dances took place as an annual festival to the Lord. Shiloh was where the Ark of the Covenant was kept, which was the place of God's presence.

Reread The Dance of David. The Lord did not rebuke David or cause any harm to Israel when they brought the Ark back to the City of David from Abinadab's house in the way the Lord prescribed, with David dancing with all his might.

We know God did not approve of the dancing in Exodus 35, for that was not dancing done in praise or worship to the Lord. However, every mention of dance that was done unto the Lord is pleasing and acceptable to Him.

Many of us have experienced the joy of watching children dance. There is something so cute and innocent about their uninhibited dance that brings us delight. Many (including myself) can also attest to the dynamic beauty of dance expressed through pure worship, whether personal or professional, to the Lord. What if dance is something that is in us from the beginning—a gift from

God? Our error lies in not recognizing the Source (or Creator) of dance. God's creation of dance, as with all things He created, was meant for our good. We also err in not recognizing the ungodly music we allow to creep into our lives as having a negative effect on us and our relationship with God.

What about performance or professional dancing as praise to the Lord? There are a handful of dance studios throughout the United States and Canada that teach dance according to God's standards. How fortunate you are if you happen to be near one! Trained dancers and choreographed dance can tell powerful stories of the Bible, be used to draw people to the Lord, and stir people to "war and contend" with worship and prayer in the spiritual realm to defeat principalities and bring spiritual breakthroughs.

Wouldn't it be wonderful if more dance studios began to glorify God through their teaching? Can you imagine how that might influence our culture and future generations? If God is causing a stirring in your heart to open such a studio, may God confirm and establish it!

When those with a heart to dance discover Psalms 149:3 and 150:4, they often breathe a big sigh of relief because they finally realize it's OK to dance in praise to the Lord. Read these Psalms and see if you can imagine and feel the joy, delight, and exuberance of praising the Lord with dance. Then take the time to dance. I dare you to; yes, now.

– 16 –

"Life's Not Fair" Dance

They send out their little ones like a flock
and their children dance.
—Job 21:11

The book of Job is thought to be one of the oldest books in the Bible. Estimated to have been written between the 6th and 4th centuries BC, it is considered a literary work of unknown authorship. Since it is a literary work, you may wonder if Job was a real or fictional character. As we dig into scripture, you will come to see that the book of Job is much more than just a literary work or an allegory.

There was a man in the land of Uz whose name was Job.
Now that man was blameless and upright;
he feared God and shunned evil.
—Job 1:1

That man was the greatest of all the people of the East.
—Job 1:3b

Was there really a land of Uz? While no discovery has yet been made of any artifacts or ancient maps showing a land of Uz, it is quite possible that someone with that name established it. Genealogies listed in the book of Genesis, chapters ten and thirty-six, cite two different people named Uz, one from the line of Shem (one of Noah's sons), and one from the Horites. Let's look first at chapter ten and the account of Shem's line of descendants.

> *Sons were also born to Shem, who was Japheth's older*
> *brother and the father of all the sons of Eber. Shem's*
> *sons were Elam, Asshur, Arpachshad, Lud and Aram.*
> *Aram's sons were Uz, Hul, Gether and Mash.*
> *—Genesis 10:21–23*

The second person by the name of Uz is noted in Genesis 36.

> *These are Dishan's sons: Uz and Aran.*
> *—Genesis 36:28*

Dishan was a son of Seir the Horite. The Horites were inhabitants of the land of Seir, where Esau traveled to and lived after growing too numerous and prosperous in possessions to reside near his brother, Jacob. Deuteronomy 2:5 tells us the Lord gave Esau the land of Seir.

The Bible does not further explain who the Horites were or their ancestry prior to Seir. Since we know that Noah's family was the only one saved out of the worldwide flood, it is certain the Horites were descendants of one of Noah's sons. We just don't know which one.

The book of Lamentations mentions the land of Uz as a dwelling place of the Edomites.

> *Rejoice and be glad, O daughter of Edom,*
> *you who dwell in the land of Uz.*
> *—Lamentations 4:21a*

Esau was the father of the Edomites, according to Genesis 36:1, 8–9, 43. This verse in Lamentations confirms Deuteronomy 2:4–5, that the Edomites occupied the land of Uz. Could it be the land of Uz is the same as the land of Seir? I do not definitively know, but along with a few other researchers, I think it is a good possibility.

Job was a man of great wealth and possessions just as Abraham, Isaac, Esau, and Jacob were.

> *He had seven sons and three daughters and his*
> *possessions were 7,000 sheep, 3,000 camels, 500 yoke of*
> *oxen and 500 female donkeys, and a very large house-*
> *hold. That man was the greatest of*
> *all the people of the East.*
> *—Job 1:2–3*

His sons held banquets, each on his own day of the week, in his own home. They invited their sisters, and they ate and drank together. After a round of banquets, Job would offer sacrifices for the sake of his children in case they had sinned. Why would he do that? First of all, he was a good father who deeply loved his family. Another hint is given in Job 2, where a dialogue occurs between the Lord and satan.

*"…And he still holds firmly to his integrity,
though you incited Me against him
to ruin him without any reason."*
—*Job 2:3c*

The narrative here is in the past tense. Had Job already experienced difficult times, tragedies, or persecutions because of satan? Here satan is again, believing that Job would curse God if His hand of protection was removed from him (Job 2:5).

God gives Job into satan's hand with one caveat: to spare his life. Complete calamity and destruction are visited on Job and his family. Through sudden enemy attacks, a fire, a raid, and a mighty wind, all of Job's children and most of the livestock and servants were killed. Job finds himself in such physical pain and agony from head-to-toe skin boils that when he is visited by three of his friends, they remain with him, silent, for seven days. Can you recall a time in your own life when a friend or family member was in such agony from an illness that you couldn't speak, but you were just there to comfort them? Were you able to even touch that sick friend, child, or other family member to comfort them? Job was in too much pain for anyone to touch or speak to him.

He finally speaks in chapter three, cursing the day he was born, but refusing to speak against God. With such horrible grief and affliction upon him, his friends assume that Job must have been hiding some secret sin that had brought this punishment. Aren't we tempted to react the same way when we see someone suffering over and over again? "It must be their fault because God is good and would not allow that to happen if this person had not sinned."

Job maintains he is innocent—because he is—and defends the Lord's goodness. However, he begins to challenge God about the way he has been treated and for his miserable life as a man. He basically declares that his suffering is unfair. He is without much hope at all. His friends presumptuously speak up to rebuke him, not giving him the comfort they came to bestow. He comes to the conclusion that the wicked are better off, for they do not experience such suffering or tragedy. In chapter twenty-one Job lists the good things the wicked have, including dance in verse eleven. The children of the wicked freely play and frolic about without a care, while Job's own children, all ten of them, were destroyed in one day, in one moment of time.

Job continues to complain and argue with God. Likely thinking his days are coming to an end, he remembers and reflects on his better days. Another young friend comes along attempting to give Job perspective and understanding. God finally speaks to Job in chapter thirty-eight, setting all things straight about who He is. Job is corrected, humbled, and in time, restored. God always restores.

> *So ADONAI blessed Job's latter days more than at his*
> *beginning. He had 14,000 sheep, 6,000 camels, 1,000*
> *yoke of oxen and 1,000 female donkeys. He also*
> *had seven sons and three daughters.*
> *—Job 42:12–13*

> *After this, Job lived 140 years; he saw his children*
> *and their children for four generations.*
> *—Job 42:16*

Job is mentioned, directly and indirectly, four times in Ezekiel 14 (written approximately in the 6th century BC) as being righteous among men, along with Noah and Daniel. He is one of only three men the Lord points to who could be delivered or saved because of his righteousness. Neither Samuel—a great priest, nor David—a man after God's own heart (both 12th century BC), were mentioned as righteous.

> *"Even if these three men—Noah, Daniel and Job—be in it, they would only deliver their own souls by their righteousness."*
> *It is a declaration of ADONAI.*
> *—Ezekiel 14:14*

How did Noah, Daniel, and Job achieve their righteousness? I do not claim to fully know, but in part, their righteousness came from their heart to obey and honor God no matter what; it was by their unwavering faith. Noah was ridiculed and humiliated by the public and his peers for building an ark as God had instructed him. Despite 100 years of persecution by society, he did as God directed him and out of all humanity at that time only he and his family were saved from the flood.

Daniel was taken into Babylonian exile and trained to serve the king. With all the pagan lifestyle and worship and the government edicts to bow to a false image, Daniel served and bowed only to God. When Daniel disobeyed the unrighteous government, the king had him sent into the lions' den for his sure demise. God intervened to spare his life by shutting the mouths of the lions.

Then we have Job. Despite losing his children, his great wealth, and his health, all in one day, he refused to curse God. In the end God restored him to double his previous position.

One of the fruits of the Spirit in Galatians 5:22–23 is patience, or long-suffering. Job, along with Noah and Daniel, are excellent examples of this fruit in times of great distress. Despite the public, governmental, personal, and physical persecutions they endured,

God considers these three men alone (outside the saving grace of Jesus Christ) righteous.

The lesson from the mention of dance in the book of Job runs deep. We cannot live by sight, assuming in our difficulties and tragedies that the wicked are better off as we watch their children dancing wild and free without a care. Rather, He would have us walk by faith, constantly trusting and submitting everything to Him.

Through His Word, we can be aware that Satan does indeed accuse us before God, just as he did with Job. But God is faithful and will work all things out for our good. He is looking for a right heart, a right spirit, and humble obedience within us. May we in our own personal struggles seek and trust God to bring us through every dark pit and into His goodness and light.

– 17 –

The Dance of Mahanaim

Come back, come back, O Shulammite! Come back, come back, that we may look upon you. Why do you gaze at the Shulammite like the dance of Mahanaim?
—Song of Songs 7:1

Can you believe this adventure we are on? There are so many mentions of dance in the Bible: spontaneous and celebratory dances, self-gratifying dances, dancing at annual festivals, dances designed to evoke a response from a god, dances to celebrate and praise the true God, and plundering army dances. Everyone including common people, warriors, a king, priests, prophets, children, and animals, dance. God even dances over His people. In Song of Songs we read about another dance, one that is only visible in the individual mind.

The song of songs of Solomon
—Song of Songs 1:1

Song of Songs, or Song of Solomon, is a short but intimately rich book; specifically, as the title indicates, it is a song. The title verse in the Orthodox Jewish Bible is "The Ultimate Song, by

Shlomo." At first glance, it displays a poetic weaving of conversation and events between two lovers. As with many books in the Bible, however, the more we study them, the richer and deeper the meanings within become.

Scholars differ in opinion as to who actually wrote this book. The Bible text also varies slightly at Song of Songs 1:1 (or the chapter title in many versions). Throughout the eight chapters, 1:1 is the only verse that mentions Solomon, which has caused controversy over the authorship of the book. The NIV reads, "Solomon's Song of Songs," indicating it was written by him or that it was his personal story. Other versions may list the song as "of Solomon," "for Solomon," "to Solomon," or "by Solomon." This leads some to believe that someone other than Solomon may have written it. I don't know of any other time when a preposition was more controversial, or if it matters much, but the lack of a clear preposition certainly keeps some people busy trying to figure out which is correct.

Other controversies include whether this poetic song is literal or fantastical. It could be a bit of both. Also, is Song of Songs meant to depict love between a man and a woman, or a deeper meaning referring to Christ and His bride? Again, it is likely that it reflects both.

Song of Songs reads a bit like a script with three players: the beloved, or bride; the lover, or groom; and the observing people, or friends. There is much intimacy and story-telling about the bride and grooms' relationship in the first five chapters. Chapter six begins with the friends of the bride asking her where her lover has gone, and she answers that he has gone down to his garden to graze his flocks and to gather lilies.

According to verse ten, it appears that the bride has gone to find him in his garden, and he speaks as she approaches. He richly praises her unique beauty in verses four through ten.

Who is this that appears like dawn? As beautiful
as the moon, bright as the sun, awesome
as an army with banners.
—Song of Songs 6:10

By the time we get to chapter seven, there is no doubt that the bride is incredibly attractive and beautiful, not only in the groom's sight, but also in the friends' views. Her friends call for her to come back so they may look upon her. In reply, her lover asks the friends why they gaze at her like the dance of Mahanaim. And so we arrive at the dance. What was this dance of Mahanaim?

According to *Strong's Expanded Exhaustive Concordance of the Bible,* Mahanaim is a town east of the Jordan. It is first mentioned in Genesis 32:3 when Jacob, with his wives, children, and possessions, parted from Laban and his relatives. Jacob secretly escaped from his father-in-law because of dishonesty and mistreatment over the previous twenty years. After three days had passed, Laban was told of their departure. He, along with other relatives, chased after them for seven days. In a dream, God warned Laban to not harm Jacob. After meeting, and a time of setting things right, they peacefully went their separate ways. As Jacob moved on from there, angels of God met him (Genesis 32:2), and Jacob gave this place its name.

Then Jacob said when he saw them, "This is God's camp,"
and he named that place Mahanaim.
—Genesis 32:3

Joshua 13:24-26 says that the place of Mahanaim was included in the land inheritance given to the tribe of Gad. Mahanaim is next mentioned in 2 Samuel 2:8. Following the death of Saul, Israel's first king, the kingdom was divided in two. Mahanaim was the town where Abner, Saul's army commander, made Saul's son Ish-bosheth king (2 Samuel 2:8). He reigned over Israel for two years; however, David was the king in Hebron over the tribe of house of Judah. Following Ish-bosheth's death, David reigned over all of Israel, and his son Solomon became king after him. Solomon had twelve officers throughout the land of Israel. Each officer in turn provided the king's food for a whole month. Ahinadab, son of Iddo, from Mahanaim, was one of the twelve officers (1 Kings 4:14). This is the last mention of the town. While we know of the city's general location based on scripture, archaeologists have not yet found definitive evidence of what happened to this town.

So we are left knowing very little about the dance of Mahanaim. Does it refer to a specific dance? Was it an annual celebration? Was it choreographed, or was it spontaneous? Given the beauty and love expressed between the lovers in the Song of Songs and the enamored friends gazing at the bride "like the dance of Mahanaim," we can only imagine the dance must have been a sight to behold.

$$- 18 -$$

A Lament

Joy has ceased in our hearts.
Our dance has turned into mourning.
—Lamentations 5:15

Praise and worship to God, expressed through dance, bring Him pleasure. We are His workmanship, His creation, with a built-in desire to move and respond to His goodness. Dance brings joy and delight and expresses strength and power, beauty and wonderment, and tender love. It is a good thing—one of the good and perfect gifts from our Father of lights (James 1:17).

For the full scope of this story, we need to go back more than 300 years to the reign of Solomon. Like Saul and the many kings who followed David, Solomon began his reign with a good heart and good intentions. Power and prestige, however, often cause people to think more highly of themselves than they should, and their influence certainly worked into Solomon's heart and mind. He loved many foreign women, who led him astray to worship their gods and turn from the Lord.

*So ADONAI became angry with Solomon, because his heart had
turned away from ADONAI, the God of Israel—who had
appeared to him twice. "So ADONAI said to Solomon:
"Since you have done this and did not keep My covenant
and My statutes that I commanded you, I will
surely tear the kingdom away from you
and give it to your servant."*
—1 Kings 11:9, 11

Though God would tear the kingdom from Solomon, for the
sake of his father, David, it would not happen until the kingdom
had passed to the hands of Solomon's son (1 Kings 11:12–13). At
that time, Israel was split into two kingdoms. Israel to the north
was led by Solomon's servant, Jeroboam, and Solomon's son, Rehoboam, retained rulership of Judah to the south.

Kings of both divisions rose and fell over many decades, and
the Lord continued to warn them through His prophets to turn
from their wicked ways and return to Him. Finally, in 2 Kings 25,
King Nebuchadnezzar and his army destroyed the city of Jerusalem and the Lord's temple and took the people of Judah into Babylonian exile.

God is a long-suffering patient God. He always warns His
people and calls them to come back to Him before following
through on His warnings. This is what He does throughout the
book of Jeremiah (as well as all the books of the prophets). He not
only warns His own people, but He also speaks of the impending
punishment He will pour out on other nations who mistreat His
people (Jeremiah 50:11-12).

Jeremiah was the Lord's prophet during the time leading up to
the destruction of Jerusalem. God's message through Jeremiah, for

the southern kingdom of Judah to repent and return to the Lord, was desperate and heartfelt. Knowing what the Lord would do if Judah did not return caused Jeremiah great sorrow, grief, and weeping over Jerusalem. In fact, he is the attributed author of Lamentations, a compilation of five laments expressing deep mourning over Jerusalem's great fall. Lamentations describes how beautiful the city was, and how it was all so suddenly lost because of those who refused to heed the voice of God.

This was a dark, disturbing period in Israel's history. Jeremiah was not comfortable speaking out God's Word because the people of that time did not want to hear anything that did not agree with their fleshly, self-focused lives. He was afraid no one would hear him, he was afraid of condemnation, and he was even afraid for his life. For bravely speaking the Lord's messages, he was mistreated, sought out to be killed, betrayed, mob-attacked, arrested, beaten, and jailed. He preached an incredibly unpopular message the people refused to hear.

In the final lament, Lamentations 5:15 speaks of the lost joy and dancing that was turned into mourning. The original word translated as *dancing* is *mâchôwl* (maw-khole'), which stems from *chûwl* (khool) or *chîyl* (kheel). These words represent a literal dance, meaning to twist or whirl in a circular or spiral manner, specifically a round dance.

Because of the people's negligence to return to the Lord's ways, forewarned-of consequences came to pass, shifting the joyful dancing into grieving. God's discipline is oh so harsh, but warranted. Here again, however, God leaves His people with the hope of restoration. Jeremiah ends this lament by asking the Lord for that restoration.

Bring us back to You, ADONAI, and we will return.
Renew our days as of old.
—Lamentations 5:21

Through Christ's death, our sins are forgiven and covered by His blood. Take a moment now to thank the Lord for your own family, ancestry, and heritage, that the past things are forgiven and that the Lord, with your cooperation, would bring complete restoration and blessing on your future generations.

– 19 –

A Time to Dance

*A time to weep and a time to laugh, a time
to mourn and a time to dance.*
—Ecclesiastes 3:4

Time both blesses and frustrates us. It provides us with structure and boundaries and is a way to balance our daily activities. We often wish we had more of it, and yet we often fail to use wisely what we already have. In Ecclesiastes, the author—Solomon, most likely—ponders the use of time and the meaning of man's activities. He surmises that much of our activity is meaningless and futile and determines the best mankind can do is to enjoy his work and the fruitfulness of it, eating and drinking, because it is the gift of God (Ecclesiastes 3:13).

Can you relate to the author's conclusion of much futility in our activities? I can. Just think of the many daily tasks we do, undo, and do again: dirty dishes, laundry, bed-making. At the office we may create and re-create weekly or monthly reports, fill and refill paper and ink. We try to appease or educate customers or clients only to do it again another day with someone else or even the same person. We set tasks and schedule reminders only to forget about them or ignore them; but then we set them again. In the field we plant, weed, harvest, and plant again. We take up hobbies and activities, get distracted from them, and take them up again.

What are the futile activities in your life? What is the fruitfulness of these activities? Is it merely to enjoy the work and eat and drink? A gift of God? I think it is as long as we have a good understanding and attitude, and have others with whom to share the activities or the fruits of them. It's about finding joy in the One who created you and placed you where you are. It's the enjoyment of having a family to work and provide for as well as to cook and clean for; the pleasures of your children growing to live productive lives of their own; the fun shared in passing the time with neighbors; and the blessing of sharing all that living with family and friends, eating and drinking.

Ecclesiastes 3:1–8 compares opposite activities: birth and death, planting and uprooting, killing and healing, tearing down and building up, weeping and laughing, mourning and dancing, scattering and gathering, embracing and refraining, finding and losing, keeping and discarding, tearing apart and mending, being silent and speaking, loving and hating, and war and peace. These are the activities of man "given to the children of men to keep them occupied" (Ecclesiastes 3:10). As indicated, the activities are not always pleasant, and relationships are difficult at times, but with wisdom you know the adversities will pass and rejoicing will come again. I love the next couple of verses, which state exactly that.

*He has made everything beautiful in its time. Moreover, He has set
eternity in their heart—yet without the possibility that
humankind can ever discover the work that God
has done from the beginning to the end. I know
that there is nothing better for them than
to rejoice and enjoy themselves
in their lifetime.*
—Ecclesiastes 3:11–12

No one can imagine the lengths God has gone to in creating a wonderful, beautiful, exciting land for us to discover and enjoy. It is the selfishness of man and the manipulation of the enemy of man's soul that destroys the joy and wonder.

Dance is one of the things God gave us to keep us occupied. We can rejoice and delight in this activity He has given us. We can praise and worship Him with dance. It is one of the good gifts from Him. The Hebrew word translated as *dance* in Ecclesiastes 3:4 is *raqad* (raw-kad'). It means to stamp, that is, to spring about (wildly or for joy). That should put a smile on your face and bring laughter to your heart.

Laughing and dancing are the opposite of weeping and mourning. Our lives will have times of grief and sorrow, but God has delighted to give us a time to wildly stamp and spring about for joy. Whether we are rejoicing in His goodness or rejoicing over an event or a victory in our lives, dancing is a good activity and use of time that pleases Him.

— 20 —

The Rejection

'We played the flute for you, but you did not dance.
We wailed, but you did not mourn.'
—Matthew 11:17

They are like children sitting in the marketplace and cal-
ling to each other, saying, 'We played the flute for you,
and you didn't dance. We sang a dirge,
and you didn't weep.
—Luke 7:32

These complimentary verses are the words of Jesus speaking to the multitudes gathered near to hear Him. He was speaking to the people of John the Baptist. At first, Jesus' words can be difficult to understand; therefore, they are often overlooked. Coming to understand them will reveal how much the Lord desires a relationship with His people and how grieved He must be when His message is rejected.

John was in prison at this time. Before his imprisonment, he had been proclaiming Jesus' arrival and calling for people to repent and prepare for His coming. His story is told well through the Scriptures, but we must seek them out from different books within the Bible for a more complete understanding.

105

*"Turn away from your sins, for the kingdom of heaven is
near!" For he is the one Isaiah the prophet spoke
about, saying, "The voice of one crying in the
wilderness, 'Prepare the way of ADONAI,
and make His paths straight.'"*
—Matthew 3:2–3

*So with many other exhortations,
John proclaimed Good News
to the people.*
—Luke 3:18

There was an obvious conflict between John, who was calling
for people to repent, and the Pharisees and Sadducees (priests and
Levites) who thought so highly of themselves that they didn't feel
they needed to repent of their sins. They did not respect John, as
noted in Matthew 3:7–12 and in John 1:19–28.

In one particular moment of ministry, John was crying out and
baptizing people who were repenting of their sins when Jesus arrived to be baptized.

*The next day, John sees Yeshua coming to him and says,
"Behold, the Lamb of God who takes
away the sin of the world!
—John 1:29*

*I did not know Him; but the One who sent me to
immerse in water said to me, 'The One on whom
you see the Ruach coming down and remaining,
this is the One who immerses in the Ruach
ha-Kodesh.' And I have seen and testified
that this is Ben-Elohim."
—John 1:33–34*

Again the next day, John was standing with two of his disciples and watched Yeshua walking by. He said, "Behold, the Lamb of God!"
—John 1:35–36

In Matthew 3:13, Jesus came to John to be baptized in the Jordan River. John's initial natural reaction was that Jesus, the Lamb of God, did not have any need to be baptized, especially by him, a mere man. However, His was not a baptism of repentance; but for our benefit, a public baptism of the Holy Spirit. Out of obedience, John baptized Christ. In that moment, when the Holy Spirit came upon Jesus in the form of a dove, and John heard God's voice from heaven, he knew without a doubt that Jesus was the Son of God (Luke 3:22).

Following Jesus' baptism, He was led by the Spirit into the wilderness to be tempted by satan. Meanwhile, John ended up in prison, and Jesus learned of it shortly thereafter.

Now when Yeshua heard that John had been handed over,
He withdrew to the Galilee.
—Matthew 4:12

Now after John was put in jail, Yeshua came into the Galilee,
proclaiming the Good News of God.
—Mark 1:14

But Herod the tetrarch—after being rebuked by John because of
Herodias, his brother's wife, and because of all the evil things
Herod had done—added even this on top of them all:
he shut up John in prison.
—Luke 3:19–20

During John's imprisonment, Jesus chose the twelve men He would closely disciple. He was teaching and performing miracles in the region. Did doubt about Jesus' nature enter John's mind while he was in prison? Was he wondering if he would ever be released? Maybe he was wrong about who Jesus was after all.

Isn't this what the enemy of our souls always does? When we are in a time of weakness and despair, he skillfully and purposefully shoots those arrows of doubt at us. If we are not grounded in our relationship with the Lord—and sometimes even if we are—our minds take a slow turn in the wrong direction.

At times, the Lord allows this testing so we can see the depth of our own faith. John's faith got a little shaky here, so he sent some of his disciples to Jesus.

> … *"Are You the Coming One, or do we look for another?"*
> —*Matthew 11:3*

Jesus told John's disciples to report to John all the miracles that were taking place and the good news that was being spread. Then He spoke about John to the crowds, who would have heard about John's question and Jesus' response. Some in the crowd were likely the doubtful priests and Levites. Since they did not believe John's message, they also had a hard time believing that Jesus had any authority from God, even though they couldn't figure out where He was getting His power from. Jesus declared John's identity and even stated the unfathomable to that crowd.

> *"And if you are willing to accept it, he is Elijah who is to come.*
> *He who has ears, let him hear!"*
> —*Matthew 11:14–15*

Next, Jesus compared that generation to children making music in the streets, both joyful and sorrowful, and calling out for a response from the people (see this chapter's two key verses). Jesus continued calling out those who refused to believe in John because he had not come "eating and drinking" —a reference to being a privileged or an important person in society. On the other hand, Jesus had come "eating and drinking" (Matthew 11:19 and Luke 7:34), but they refused to believe in Him because, ironically, He ate and drank, but did so with sinners and tax collectors, which, in the eyes of the people, made Him a glutton and a drunkard.

Jesus then denounced the towns where He had performed many miracles. Despite the testimonies of the former Old Testament prophets being fulfilled by John and Jesus, and miracles done by Jesus, the people still denied that John was the one prophesied about. John was the one sent to announce Jesus' arrival and that Jesus was the Son of God. Rather, John and Jesus were treated as unimportant children. The leaders did not respond to the good news by dancing to the music, nor did they mourn, because they couldn't see their own coming destruction.

What an awful testimony to what was happening at that time. Jesus' heart was for the good of all people. He desired to heal them, teach them, bless them, and show them the heart of His Father. Yet they rejected Him.

Jesus' heart is the same toward us today. He desires that we receive His gift of healing, learn from His teachings, receive His many blessings, and accurately see the heart of His Father through relationship with Him. Spend time seeking Him today and respond to the music and the call.

– 21 –

A Birthday Celebration

But when Herod's birthday celebration came, the daughter of Herodias danced before them and pleased Herod.
—Matthew 14:6

When the daughter of Herodias came in and danced, she pleased Herod and those reclining with him. And the king said to the girl, "Ask me for whatever you want, and I'll give it to you!"
—Mark 6:22

Following Jesus' forty-day wilderness experience, He heard that John had been imprisoned. John's message to the world was for all people to repent and be baptized, preparing their hearts to receive their coming Messiah and King.

Herod the Tetrarch (a lesser king) of the Galilean and Perean area (the region from south of Galilee to the Jordan) had married his brother's wife, Herodias. John advised Herod that this marriage was not appropriate, which made Herodias bitter toward John. She manipulated Herod so that he would put John in prison. She really wanted him killed, but Herod knew the people revered John as a prophet, and he enjoyed listening to John speak, so Herod looked out for John.

When a large birthday celebration was held for Herod, Herodias encountered her opportunity to get rid of John. This grand banquet was a joyful celebration with many important people in attendance. The dance by Herodias' daughter was likely a planned part of the event. We are not told her age, but since she was called a girl in Mark 6:22, she must have been young.

Herod enjoyed her dance so much that he offered her whatever she wanted, up to half of his kingdom (Mark 6:23). Not knowing what to ask for in response to Herod's offer, she went to her mother (another indication of her youth), who told her to ask for John's head. Herod was distressed over this request, but due to the verbal oath he spoke while in the company of high officials and military leaders, he ordered John's immediate execution. John's disciples came and took care of his body and then informed Jesus that John was dead.

News of this man named Jesus traveled quickly throughout the region and back to Herod. It would have been hard for him not to hear, as the wife of his finance minister was a supporter of Jesus and His disciples (Luke 8:3). He spoke with incredible wisdom, often using soul-convicting parables. He cast unclean spirits from people and healed multitudes of people. Many thought He was the reincarnation of John, Elijah, or some other ancient prophet (Luke 9:19).

Herod heard all that was happening and thought this man must be John raised from the dead (Matthew 14:1–2). Whether this instilled hope or fear in him, we are not told; maybe it was both.

Regarding the girl's dance, was it a good dance or a bad dance? Was it appropriate or inappropriate? All we are told is that Herodias' daughter danced at Herod's birthday celebration and it pleased those in attendance. I assume she was attractive and talented. She danced well, and it was likely a lovely thing.

There is nothing wrong with a beautiful dance at a birthday celebration. However, through this particular dance, satan found an opportunity to work through Herodias' selfish heart. I doubt Herod saw this event unfolding the way it did, for he was grieved, but he also had a position, an ego, and a reputation to uphold among the guests which required him to follow through with his generous word, the result of which was John's death.

Life is a gift from God. He commanded that joyful feasts and celebrations be held throughout the seasons and years because He wants us to remember and rejoice in His goodness and provision for His children. Does He not also delight when we celebrate and honor one another's birthdays, weddings, and other lifetime milestones? It is the Lord who brings these things to pass in our lives. Let us celebrate to the glory of God.

– 22 –

The Great Rejoicing

*"Now his older son was out in the field. And as he came
near the house, he heard music and dancing."*
—Luke 15:25

The final specific mention of dance in the Bible is spoken in a parable by Jesus Himself. It is another wonderful scene and evidence of God's joy and approval of dancing.

Jesus was traveling from Galilee to Jerusalem (a journey of about seventy miles) where He would celebrate Passover with His disciples just before His betrayal and crucifixion. Great crowds of people were following Him everywhere He went.

*And He continued on His journey through the towns
and villages, teaching and making His way to Jerusalem.*
—Luke 13:22

While staying and dining at various homes along the way, He taught in synagogues and to the crowds. While in Capernaum (a town in the Galilee region), the crowds unsuccessfully tried to talk Him into staying with them.

But He said to them, "I must proclaim the Good News of the kingdom of God to the other towns also. It was for this purpose I was sent."
—Luke 4:43

As news of Jesus spread, the crowds that followed Him grew. There were those who were amazed by Him, many who sought to be healed, and those who wanted Him gone. It was to this last group that He pointedly shared three important parables. The Pharisees and Torah scholars despised Jesus for associating with tax collectors and sinners. He spoke these parables directly to them about the good news of the kingdom of God.

The first parable was that of the lost sheep. If one sheep is lost from a herd of 100, would not the shepherd leave the 99 and search for the one lost? Once found, would not the shepherd and those around him rejoice that the lost one was found?

"I tell you, in the same way there will be more joy in heaven over one repenting sinner than over the ninety-nine righteous people who have no need of repentance."
—Luke 15:7

Next was the same illustration in the parable of a woman who lost a silver coin. Even though she had nine other silver coins, she and her friends rejoiced when she found the one that was lost.

"In the same way, I tell you, there is joy in the presence of the angels of God over one sinner who repents."
—Luke 15:10

Finally, Jesus explained the kingdom of God in terms of humanity, relating what is commonly known as the parable of the prodigal son. It is described as follows.

A wealthy man who owned fields, animals, and servants, had two sons. The younger son got the idea that city living was the better life, so he asked his father to give him his inheritance. He planned to move on to a more exciting life. The son quickly squandered the inheritance and found meager work feeding pigs in the field of a local citizen. At this point, he was so poor that the pigs were better off than he was. Regaining some sense and logic, he decided to humbly return to his father and offer to be a servant, for his foolish behavior certainly would not be worthy of the status of a son.

The father likely knew this son would run into many challenges, but he also knew the most loving thing to do would be to allow his son to choose his own way of life while hanging onto the hope that he would return someday. Hope did not disappoint, and while the son was still a long way off, the father saw him returning. The father quickly told his servants to prepare a lavish celebration for his son's return. It didn't matter what the son had done while he was away. What was important was the return.

The older brother had been working hard in the fields. When he approached the house—no doubt, sweaty and tired—he heard music and dancing. The servants informed him that his brother had returned. Many of us would have the same reaction as the older brother—he was aggravated. Here he was, faithfully working for his father day in and day out. He knew and lived with his father's heartache over his younger brother running off to a far city. Then, when he decided to show up, he got a party? How unjust is that?

But that is the heart of The Father—our Father. He knows the curious and stubborn selfishness of our hearts, the distractions of the world, and the enemy's enticements of our souls. He is omniscient, omnipotent, and omnipresent. He is patient, that is, long-suffering. His own perfect Son, Yeshua, intercedes for us, His Holy Spirit guides and encourages us (even leading others to pray for us), and His angels minister to us to draw us back to the right path. He delights to restore us.

> *"Then the father said to him, 'Son, you are always with*
> *me, and everything that is mine is yours. But it was*
> *right to celebrate and rejoice, because this brother of*
> *yours was dead but has come back to life!*
> *He was lost, but is found.'"*
> —Luke 15:31–32

At a point in my life, I was lost and then found. You too were once lost and then found (or I pray that if you are lost, you will be found). Let's revel and be festive with the Father. The heavens rejoice and so should we when one who was lost comes home.

PART TWO

God's Inexhaustible Word

– 1 –

Discovering Biblical Dance

*It is the glory of God to conceal a matter
and the glory of kings to search it out.*
—Proverbs 25:2

I had been diligently reading the Bible for decades, but I didn't know much about what it said regarding dance. It wasn't until I was released into dancing for the Lord that I began to study what the Word says about it. Finding multiple mentions of dance in the Bible, I dug deeper, and the Word came alive. I discovered that as there are different types of dance, there are also about as many different circumstances resulting in dance. Much can be lost in translation, and that's why it's such a wonderful thing when the Lord stirs your heart to seek Him more, to look into the deeper meanings of His Word.

Take a peek at the Definitions of Dance in the Appendix section. Listed there are the Hebraic or Aramaic, and Greek words the Bible uses that are translated to some form of the English word *dance*. Read through these eight listings and see if you can distinguish which one more accurately describes David's dance versus the dances of Shiloh, the marauders dance, and the dance of Herodias' daughter.

Let's look at the variety of dance in God's holy Word. Miriam's dance in Exodus 15:20 included other people. Besides herself, the scripture says that all the women went out after her with tambourines (specifically timbrels—small hand drums) and with dancing. The Hebrew word for *dancing* is *m^echôlâh* (mek-o-law'), the feminine form of *mâchôwl* (maw-khole'), which is a very general form of dance.

I imagine that Miriam burst into spontaneous dance over God's mighty act of bringing them through the sea on dry ground and then destroying the Egyptian army when they tried to pass through in pursuit. God's chosen people had sudden and complete freedom from Egypt, and Miriam exuberantly drew the women to join her in celebratory worship. I imagine them spontaneously dancing individually as well as in groups, or possibly dancing the familiar steps of something they all knew by tradition.

Maybe you've seen artwork depicting Miriam with a handful of other women, dancing with tambourines in their hands. Artwork sometimes helps our imaginative processes, and other times it may cause us to carry an untrue picture in our minds. Miriam was part of an enormous number of people who left Egypt.

Then Bnei-Yisrael journeyed from Rameses to Succoth,
about 600,000 men on foot, as well as children. Also a
mixed multitude went up with them…
—Exodus 12:37–38

Think of the number of able-bodied men on foot, and add to that number their wives and children. Some may have ridden on animals or in carts. The Word also states that a mixed multitude of people from other nations or ethnicities chose to join them in leaving Egypt. Estimates of the number of people who left Egypt exceed 2,000,000. Visualize the multitudes of dancing women, even men and children joining in, rejoicing and glorifying God with their hand drums, singing, shouting, cheering, and dancing. How awesome that must have been.

The dances of Shiloh (Judges 21:21, 23), where the annual festival to the Lord was held, were a different kind of dance. The original Hebrew word for dance in these verses is *chûwl* (khool) or *chîyl* (kheel), which means to twist or whirl in a circular or spiral fashion in dance. This could have been a folk-type dance or a spontaneous dance. Imagine if today's churches held annual festivals with dancing in celebration to the Lord. I'm sure some do, but what if more did? It's a pattern that could richly bless families and communities.

David's famous dance was a whirling dance. The Hebrew word used for *dance* in 2 Samuel 6:14 and 16 is *kârar* (kaw-rar'). David's dance is also described in 1 Chronicles 15:29 by the Hebrew word *raqad* (raw-kad'). In addition to whirling around, he was wildly stamping and springing about with great joy. Imagine that. How he loved the Lord, and how excited he was that the Lord was favoring them in that moment. Surely, his exuberance filled the others with awe and joy, as well.

The dance of Herodias' daughter (Matthew 14:6, Mark 6:22, Luke 7:32) is described by the Greek word *orchéomai* (or-kheh'-om-ahee), which was likely a choreographed dance. Had you ever thought of this particular dance as being choreographed? It makes sense. This was a large birthday party for Herod. A lot of planning would have had to be done for such an event, and it may have included a skilled, choreographed dance. Compare it to a planned dance for a special event at your church, a school or dance studio performance, an evening at the local ballet, or some other formal affair.

By studying the scriptures and spending time with the Lord, we can gain not only a whole new revelatory understanding of the depth of His Word, His pleasure, and His heart toward us when we worship and celebrate Him in dance, but we can even gain a glimpse of dancing in the heavenlies of eternity. There is dancing in Heaven? Definitely!

– 2 –

Digging Deeper

*All scripture is inspired by God and useful for teaching,
for reproof, for restoration, and for training in righteousness, so that the person belonging to God may be capable, fully equipped for every good deed.*
—2 Timothy 3:16–17

God's Word is inexhaustible. The more you read the Bible, the richer it becomes. It is your anchor for life and source for discovering God's love for you, His plan for you, His provision for you, and His future for you. It is truly filled with everything you need to live a full and abundant life.

In the workplace, an employee in an entry-level position gains knowledge and skill through showing up and doing the assigned tasks the position requires. Over time, the entry-level employee acquires new information and takes on heavier responsibilities, leading to promotion.

The same is true of familial life. We begin as babies, learning how to eat and move about, living a life of discovery. We then transition from babies to children and then to young adults. Then we transition again from young adults into more mature adults. Each passage brings new discoveries and responsibilities. Whether we have children of our own or not, we will teach and influence others coming alongside and behind us in life's amazing journey.

The process of learning about and knowing God through His Word is similar. We begin with reading select chapters and verses and gradually expand to reading the entire Bible from Genesis to Revelation. Then we read it again, possibly several more times, and start researching the scriptures more deeply. It takes continued diligence to seek God and grow through the reading of His Word, but His promise is true—we will find Him if we continue to seek Him. If you struggle to read the Bible regularly, ask the Lord to stir the desire in you to know Him more through His Word. Ask Him for wisdom and understanding.

But if any of you lacks wisdom, let him ask of God who
gives to all without hesitation and without reproach;
and it will be given to him.
—Jacob (James) 1:5

In a world where personal pleasure and busyness are favored over a quiet and simple life (Micah 6:8, 1 Thessalonians 4:11), God's help is necessary for achieving the discipline of making time for His Word. If you do not give up, the revelations and insights that God will show you through His Word are like opening new treasures every day.

When I began dancing publicly for the Lord, I started with the use of flags. Being in front of people was definitely outside my comfort zone, but the flags provided a sense of coverage. The focus of movement would be on the flags, not on myself. Without fully understanding what I was doing or why, I knew the call was on my life—He had personally spoken to me and He had asked me to dance.

After a couple of years of watching other flag worshipers at church and on internet teaching ministries, I found a Christian dance company that offered online courses. During that amazing year of study, I learned not so much the "how-to's" of dance, but how to search and study the scriptures related to the gift of dance. I learned to focus my growth in His Word, adding in prayer, and learning to hear His voice regarding the gift. I learned to seek and trust Him to teach me how He wanted me to dance. These were invaluable lessons that drew me deeper into His Word, His presence, and His gift of the call.

Make every effort to present yourself before God as tried
and true, as an unashamed worker cutting a straight
path with the word of truth.
—2 Timothy 2:15

Use the Hebrew and Greek definitions in the back of this book to whet your appetite for study. As the Lord leads you to go deeper into His Word, make the time to read the full definitions and explanations from a concordance or an online resource. It will greatly expand your understanding of the Scriptures.

There will be periods in which you may feel you are not making progress because you are not yet understanding what the scriptures are trying to teach. You're not alone. Even Jesus' closest disciples struggled to understand what He wanted them to grasp. Do not give up. God will reveal it to you, if not now, then at a later moment of the Lord's choosing.

Then He opened their minds to understand the Scriptures...
—*Luke 24:45*

His timing for things pertaining to your life is perfect. Continue seeking Him and His ways.

– 3 –

The Foundations of Praise

Praise ADONAI, for ADONAI is good.
Sing praises to His Name, for it is delightful.
—Psalm 135:3

Dig, dig, dig. Dig into the Word. There are treasures within that the Lord is waiting with delight for you to uncover and explore. Before discovering why we are to praise Him, let's learn what the word means. It's not as easy as you might initially think. Sure, you can look it up in the dictionary, and most likely you will easily understand and agree with the basic meanings therein. However, English was not the original language of the Holy Bible; Hebrew, Aramaic, and Greek were.

The English word *praise*, including its various forms and tenses, appears over 300 times in the Bible. These instances of the word *praise* come from nineteen different Hebraic/Aramaic, and Greek words. Do these nineteen words all have the same simple meaning to be translated as "praise?"

Praise is both a noun and a verb. Merriam-Webster.com defines it as an expression of approval or commendation; worship; value, merit, given to one that is praised. As a verb, it means to express a favorable judgment of, or commend; to glorify (a god or saint) especially by the attribution of perfections; to express praise.

Let's look at the mentions of praise in Psalm 135:3 above, as well as in Psalms 149 and 150 related to dancing.

Let them praise His name with dancing. Let them sing praises to Him with tambourine and harp.
—Psalm 149:3

Praise Him with tambourine and dance. Praise Him with string instruments and flute.
—Psalm 150:4

The Hebrew word for *praise* in these two verses is *hâlal* (haw-lal'). The explanation of *hâlal* in *New Strong's Expanded Exhaustive Concordance of the Bible* takes up a whole column in the 8.5" x 11", two-inch thick, too-many-pages-to-count (with a font so small some of you may need a magnifying glass). Very generally and simply, it means to be clear (originally in sound, but usually of color); to shine; to make a show, to boast; to be (clamorously) foolish; to rave, to celebrate; also to stultify (to make foolish). This explanation is much more descriptive than the English definition for praise; don't you think?

Using your imagination with that description, how would you dance for the Lord in praise, or rather *hâlal*, to Him? How does the understanding of the definition of *hâlal* alter your thinking of what is (or what you may have been taught is not) acceptable praise to the Lord?

Keep reading your concordance, and you will discover that *hâlal* is the root of the word *Hallelujah*—the Hebrew expression that means "praise to God," or more technically, "Let us praise (*hâlal*) God (*Yah*)."

Let's look at a few more examples.

After singing the Hallel, they went out to the
Mount of Olives.
—*Mark 14:26*

Other popular Bible versions may use the word(s) "song of praise" or "hymn" instead of Hallel. In any case, the original Greek word for hymn is *humneo* (hoom-neh'-o), which means to sing a religious ode; by implication to celebrate (God) in song. Notice that the versions using the word Hallel capitalize it, which indicates a specific song or "song of praise." Historical Jewish resources explain that Hallel refers to singing Psalms 113–118 at the Passover celebration, and indeed, the setting of Mark 14:26 is the Passover. Jesus also said to His disciples as they reclined for the meal that He had eagerly desired to eat Passover with them before He suffered (Luke 22:15).

Jesus was "eager" to eat with them. The Greek word for *eager* (or *desire* in some versions) is *epithumia,* which refers to a great desire, passionate longing, or eagerness. He knew His suffering was imminent and that He would not eat the Passover with them again until it is celebrated in the kingdom of God.

Leading up to this time, Passover was a feast He would annually celebrate with his disciples, his friends. Knowing what you know now about the Hallel, and *hâlal,* did they sing a nice, pleasant, or somber hymn, or did they sing joyously and raucously, clapping, shouting praises, maybe even stomping and dancing, glorifying God?

*You turned my mourning into dancing, You removed
my sackcloth and clothed me with joy. So my glory will
sing to You and not be silent. ADONAI my God,
I will praise You forever.*
—Psalm 30:12–13

In verse thirteen, *praise* originates from the Hebrew word *zâmar* (zaw-mar'), which means to make music on an instrument, possibly even be accompanied by voice. We also see in verse twelve that dancing went along with this musical form of praise.

*Why are you downcast, O my soul? Why are you murmuring
within me? Hope in God, for I will yet praise Him,
the salvation of my countenance and my God.*
—Psalm 42:12

*Why are you downcast, O my soul? Why are you murmuring
within me? Hope in God, for I will yet praise Him,
the salvation of my countenance.*
—Psalm 43:5

These two nearly identical verses from the Psalms reveal that praising the Lord can shift our countenance (facial expression) from being downcast to having hope. The Hebrew word for *praise* in these instances is *yâdâh*, which means to hold out or to extend the hand(s) vertically or horizontally to give thanks, laud, or praise. When we extend our hands to the Lord in worship, even in dance, it is *yâdâh*. The next time you are feeling down or discouraged, choose to sing or dance with hands extended, and see if your countenance will change as it did for David.

I will praise God's Name with a song,
and magnify Him with praise.
—Psalm 69:31

The dead do not praise ADONAI, nor do any who go
down into silence. But we—we will bless ADONAI
both now and forever. Halleluyah!
—Psalm 115:17–18

Hâlal (previously described) is the praise expressed in the verses above. When David wrote Psalm 69:31, he stated in the preceding verse that He was afflicted and in pain. By dwelling on the Lord and His salvation, David overcame his troubles and was able to greatly praise Him—if not physically, at least in his heart.

Psalm 115:17–18 contrasts the praise of those who are dead with those who have everlasting life. The dead do not make a clear and certain sound. They do not praise to shine, make a show, boast, be clamorously foolish, rave, or celebrate. How wonderful it is that we can! For all that He is and for all that He does for us, we will bless and praise the Lord.

He has raised up a horn for His people, a praise for all
His kedoshim, for the children of Israel—
a people near to Him. Halleluyah!
—Psalm 148:14

This praise is *t^ehillâh* (teh-hil-law'). *T^ehillâh* comes from the word *hâlal*, as a laudation, or specifically a hymn. *T^ehillâh* means glory, praise, song of praise, or praiseworthy deeds. It describes a quality or attribute of a person or thing. The praise in this verse is a noun, referring back to a horn. What (or who) is this horn that the Lord raised up? What does "horn" mean in this verse? The Hebrew word for *horn* is *qeren* (keh'-ren). *Strong's Concordance* lists two of the several meanings as follows: a ray (of light); and figuratively, power.

Jesus is described as a horn of salvation in 2 Samuel 22:3 and Luke 1:69. Jesus is the light of the world (John 8:12), and He is power. God raised Him up for His people, for you, and for me. I want Him ever present in my life. How about you? Let Him be a horn and a praise for you.

Take a few minutes to meditatively read Psalm 148. It is a wonderful Psalm to ponder in your heart. Note that there are two "Halleluyahs" (Let us praise God), ten "praises" (*hâlal*), and one "praise" (*t^{e}hillâh*, verse fourteen). This Psalm clearly calls all creation to praise God and to praise the One He raised up so we could be near to Him.

How wonderful is God's Word! Grab a notebook and study all the nineteen Hebrew and Greek words for *praise*. May your study make you want to praise the Lord with dancing.

Let everything that has breath praise ADONAI. Halleluyah!
—Psalm 150:6

– 4 –

The Depths of Rejoicing

But let all who take refuge in You rejoice! Let them al-
ways shout for joy! You will shelter them and they
exult—those who love Your Name.
—Psalm 5:12

Similar to the word *praise*, the word *rejoice* also has a deeper, richer meaning in its original language. In its many forms, it is mentioned in the Bible approximately 286 times. Stemming from only the present tense—*rejoice*—twelve Hebrew/Aramaic words and six Greek words are translated into English as *rejoice*. Some of the more commonly used original words are included in Definitions of Rejoice in the Appendix. Let's look at some specific examples from the Word.

Yet will I triumph in ADONAI, I will rejoice
in the God of my salvation!
—Habakkuk 3:18

Sing aloud O daughter of Zion! Shout in triumph,
O Israel! Rejoice and exult wholeheartedly,
O daughter of Jerusalem!
—Zephaniah 3:14

The Hebraic word for *rejoice* in both of these verses is *'âlaz* (aw-laz'), which means to jump for joy, exult (be joyful, rejoice, triumph). These descriptive words indicate movement of the body as well as the heart. In the verse from Zephaniah, it is the Lord, speaking through Zephaniah the prophet, who is calling His chosen people to rejoice, to respond to Him. The reason for rejoicing is found in the next verse, Zephaniah 3:15, because He "has taken away your punishments" and "turned back your adversary." In verse seventeen, it is revealed that the Lord also dances, or rejoices, over us!

As you read scriptures from the Old Testament, the promises of God's people are also promises for you. Romans 10:11–13 and Ephesians 2:11–22 describe how the foreigners (or Gentiles) are joined together with the Jews and saved through trust, faith, and proclamation in and by the blood of Jesus Christ. Ephesians 3:6 calls believing Gentiles joint heirs and fellow members of the promise in Messiah Yeshua. All who believe in Him can look at and take Zephaniah 3:14–18 personally. God calls *you* to rejoice for the good things He has done. He has turned away our adversary as well as our punishments. Out of His love and goodness, He redeems and restores. As little children, we can be free in Him.

> *But let all who take refuge in You rejoice! Let them always shout for joy! You will shelter them and they exult — those who love Your Name.*
> *—Psalm 5:12*

Do you take refuge in the Lord? Do you love His name? David proclaims you are allowed to rejoice, or *sâmach* (saw-makh'); you are to brighten up, be gleesome; express a spontaneous emotion or extreme happiness accompanied by dancing, and singing, as if you are at a feast or festival.

Have you ever been in a time of praise and worship in a crowded sanctuary or auditorium where people are jumping up and down during an upbeat song? If not, why? Who taught you that you should never be in a place of that type of worship? You express these actions at a concert or sporting event, right? So why not express this kind of exuberance toward God? Jumping for joy is dancing and rejoicing before the Lord. How do you "shout for joy" without lifting your hands and arms? It is nearly impossible to express such emotion without moving your body.

Also the foreigners who join themselves to ADONAI, to minister to Him, and to love the Name of ADONAI, and to be His servants—all who keep from profaning Shabbat, and hold fast to My covenant—these I will bring to My holy mountain, and let them rejoice in My House of Prayer.
—Isaiah 56:6–7

This one is worth rereading and meditating on the words. The Lord will let the foreigners (Gentiles) who chose to follow, love, and serve Him, rejoice in His house of prayer. Other Bible versions may translate this specific portion as "give them joy," or "make them joyful." All three words: *rejoice, joy,* and *joyful* are from *sâmach* (described in the previous section).

I want to briefly discuss what it means to keep and to keep from profaning the Shabbat, the Sabbath. I do not want you to think we are under the law or the old covenant, and therefore we must honor the Sabbath as was strictly required. Jesus came with a new covenant, the covenant of perfect love. We are no longer required to keep the Sabbath from Friday evening to Saturday evening. If some honor the Lord in this way, that is perfectly acceptable because they do it to honor the Lord. It is also acceptable to honor the Lord on Sunday or on any and every day.

One person esteems one day over another while another judges every day alike. Let each be fully convinced in his own mind. The one who observes that day does so to the Lord.
—Romans 14:5–6

This may be a good time to review Romans 14 and 15, where Paul teaches about unity among all believers and allowing each the freedom to choose how to honor Him. Do not judge your brother or sister. We are all at different stages of our journeys, constantly learning and growing in wisdom and understanding in the circumstances the Lord has us in. We are to seek peace with one another. The Lord has given each of us different gifts in order to accomplish many different things. We can fully function as His body only by accepting the various gifts and choosing to live in unity.

These next three verses describe rejoicing, which comes from the Greek word *agalliáō* (ag-al-lee-ah'-o). It means to jump for joy and exult. *Exult* means to be extremely joyful, to rejoice greatly, to leap for joy. A few synonyms for exult include glory, jubilate, rejoice, and triumph.

"Rejoice and be glad, for your reward in heaven is great! For in the same way they persecuted the prophets who were before you."
—Matthew 5:12

And my spirit greatly rejoices in God, my Savior.
—Luke 1:47

*Let us rejoice and be glad and give the glory to Him! For
the wedding of the Lamb has come, and His bride has
made herself ready, she was given fine linen to wear,
bright and clean! For the fine linen is
the righteous deeds of the kedoshim.*
—Revelation 19:8–9

Remember a time in your life when you finally overcame a trying circumstance or challenge. Think of a mother of grown children, who, after waiting many years, finds out she is going to be a grandmother for the first time. Imagine a movie scene of an underrated sports team finally triumphing over a larger-than-life opponent. The resulting rejoicing is *agalliáō*, physically jumping and leaping, much like a wild dance.

As you can see from these examples, and as you will see when you look at the definitions in the back of this book, *rejoice* is not just a word that was spoken to honor the Lord or a word to reflect the condition of the heart and mind. Rather, *rejoice* is a very active word representing joyful physical reactions.

Before moving on, I encourage you once again to be aware of word meanings as you read the Bible and be willing to dig deeper into God's Word. *Celebrate* (as mentioned in Part One, Chapter 4: Dances of Shiloh), and *worship* are words that may also reflect dance in portions of scripture. Look them up and let God speak to you in a new and more meaningful way. As you read the Word, I hope your thoughts and visions are forever altered as to how King David and so many others loved and related to the Lord.

PART THREE

Dancing for the Lord

– 1 –

God's Call

Faithful is the One who calls you —
and He will make it happen!
—1 Thessalonians 5:24

When God calls us into a specific gifting, role, or position, we may not feel qualified or understand the fullness of it, but it is a done deal as far as He is concerned. God's call upon His people is always grand; that is, it is beyond what we consider ourselves capable of.

Just like many people in the Bible, we often do not grasp the Lord's vision for our lives at the moment it is revealed. Sarah laughed when she heard that she was to bear a child in her very old age. Moses perceived a lack in his speaking skills, so he did not feel qualified to go before Pharaoh and speak for the release of his kinsmen. Gideon did not feel he was a strong and courageous warrior, so he asked God for multiple signs of confirmation. Saul declared to Samuel that he was from the least of the clans of the tribe of Benjamin, and at the age of forty, he hid among the baggage when he was about to be set as king over Israel. Jeremiah thought he was too young and ill-equipped to serve as the Lord's prophet. In each of these lives, however, God knew what He had put within them and the great things they would achieve. He knows the same about you. God has purposes for your life that you can't even imagine yet, purposes that He placed within you at the time He first thought of you.

Regardless of what a person does for a living, as believers in Christ, we are all called to live a life dedicated to the Lord and to spread the gospel. Each of us is responsible for our personal relationship with Him and for growing in our understanding of the scriptures, which were written to assist us in building up the church, equipping and encouraging one another, and using the gifts of the five-fold ministry (missionaries, prophets, evangelists, preachers, and teachers). We do these things in the midst of living our daily lives wherever we go in all the earth. The Lord created us to minister in a great variety of ways in order to reach a great variety of people. When you give Him your attention and devotion, He will lead you and grow you, continually expanding your skills and ability to walk right into His specific call for your life.

Even more biblical examples illustrate that you are, or will be, strategically placed. Abraham was a wealthy shepherd, who, by his obedience to the Lord, left his extended family to go to a place the Lord would show him. He did many great things, and, in his old age, became the father of many nations. Through his one promised son, the twelve tribes of Israel were born. After young Joseph received a dream indicating he would have great authority, he was sold into slavery and spent years in prison. Yet he was eventually established as second in command of the kingdom. God used him to save his family and many others from famine. Esther was a beautiful, young, orphaned Hebrew, who became queen of a vast empire. Did she know the Lord would place her in a position to save her people? Mary was a young woman tending to her family and daily life, betrothed to be married, with no idea that she would birth the Savior of the world until an angel came to visit her. Paul was a tentmaker by trade—a skill that gave him the freedom to travel as a preacher and teacher of the gospel, which was his kingdom ministry. Trust the Lord in your own life that He knows where you live and what you do. Through your obedience to Him, He will move you into position to live out His calling on your life.

When you discover His call for you, God will also determine the timing of its release. Abraham and Sarah waited 25 years for God's promise of a son to be realized. Joseph's dreams took decades to come to pass. The Israelites were promised deliverance from Egypt but had to wait 430 years. After David's anointing, it would be another 13 years before he became king. Jesus waited 30 years for His specific time of ministry. It took 16 years from God's call on my life for it to be publicly released.

Let time take its course. Few people are thrust suddenly into ministry. It often takes time and effort, study and practice, and a period of gaining experience. Wait upon the Lord (both waiting and listening, as well as waiting on and serving). You are in training. Be patient. Submit to Him. Search the scriptures in relation to your call. Be faithful to where He already has you (family, work, etc.). He is setting things into place for your success.

Jumping ahead of His timing will likely lead to setbacks and disappointments. Even though you may feel time is running out, if you are faithful to Him, He will accomplish His will through you, and you will release the honor and glory to Him that He created you to bring forth. God has not forgotten you and will bring to pass the things He has planned for you as long as you seek Him and increasingly live a godly lifestyle.

Hopefully, many will be excited for you as you grow in your gift. They may willingly share their specific ideas about what you must now do to grow in your calling. Cautiously weigh those voices. God does speak through others, but their messages should always confirm what He has already spoken to you. Guard your heart and pray that you will not allow yourself to be tempted to take matters into your own hands in order to elevate yourself more quickly. Well-meaning or not, even Jesus' brothers tried to get Him to make Himself known before His time (John 7:2–4).

> *Therefore submit to God. But resist the devil and he will*
> *flee from you. Draw near to God and He will draw*
> *near to you. Humble yourselves in the sight of*
> *ADONAI, and He shall lift you up.*
> *—Jacob (James) 4:7–8, 10*

Also know that not everyone will understand your calling. Others may think, and even comment, that you are not equipped or capable. They may be right! But the Lord, rather than man, knows what He has placed within you that has not yet been awakened. Regardless of what others think, go ahead and dance (or write, speak, create, teach, heal). Listen to God rather than man.

> *Your eyes saw me when I was unformed, and in Your*
> *book were written the days that were formed—*
> *when not one of them had come to be.*
> *—Psalm 139:16*

The Lord said of Jeremiah (and His thoughts are the same toward you), I know the plans I have for you (Jeremiah 29:11). Give up your control and your thoughts of the perfect timing for growing and releasing your gifting and let God unfold His plans for your life. Press on to know Him and hear His voice. He is never in a rush when it comes to developing you.

There is nothing wrong with small (or slow, or late) beginnings. Zechariah 4:8–10 tells how the eyes of the Lord rejoice at small beginnings. You may have much to learn and grow in. Keep abiding in the Lord, and you will bear much fruit (John 15:5). His promises are true.

– 2 –

Gift Development

*As each one has received a gift, use it to serve
one another, as good stewards of the
many-sided grace of God.*
—1 Peter 4:10

Don't you just love to receive unexpected gifts, especially ones that are so well thought out, customized specifically for your taste and style, and given by someone important in your life, or because you are special in a unique way to the gift-giver? That's how discovering God's gift in you should be. Find yourself amazed that He planned this for you from before the beginning of time. It is His delight to bless you, and then, for His glory, for you to bless Him and others by using that gift.

What is the first thing a child will do with a gift chosen and tailored just for him or her? Play with it! Be free to learn and enjoy this gift the Lord has hidden within until the proper time. Watch others when they step into their gifts and see how they are so excited, happy as children, to dance or flag for the Lord. It is all they want to do, and it gives them great pleasure. They are so energized to operate in the gift that, at first, it may look like it's *all about them*, and it is! Rejoice with them; they have discovered something so very special from the Lord. They won't do it perfectly. Most won't fully understand what they are doing or why, but that is all right. You go and do the same.

> *But Yeshua called for them, saying, "Let the little children come to Me and do not hinder them, for the kingdom of God belongs to such as these."*
> *—Luke 18:16*

Now, I know this verse is talking about little, or young, children, but aren't we all children of God, told to come to Him with child-like faith? Rejoice in the Lord and His love toward all His children! He receives us in our humble states and respective beginnings (Zechariah 4:10).

With our gifts or talents from the Lord, however, we should not remain as children. Sure, there will be many spontaneous moments to respond with child-like freedom, but the Lord also calls His children into maturity.

> *Do not neglect the spiritual gift within you which was given to you through prophecy with the laying on of hands of the elders. Practice these things—be absorbed in them, so that your progress may be clear to all.*
> *—1 Timothy 4:14–15*

Growing in your calling means you need to learn about the gift God has given you and how to operate in it. What is the Lord's purpose for dance through you? How will you accomplish what He has set before you, and how will you handle the gift given to you? This doesn't mean you simply need to dance more (although that never hurts), but rather seek Him for guidance so that He is glorified through your actions. A teen or adult that continues to act like a toddler does not bring honor to the parents, but one that is teachable brings pleasure and joy.

Maybe you grew up taking dance lessons. Depending on whether you gained skills in secular dance or liturgical dance will make a difference, for those two arenas of dance are very different. One is used for entertainment and selfish desires, while the other is used to bring glory to God. Those who learned to dance in the secular world and are later called by God often walk away from dance for a period of time in order to find God's purposes. A process of unlearning and relearning may need to take place, but do not give up on dancing! There are Christian dance companies and theaters in need of your skill.

The dancer with no previous experience is not necessarily a clean slate, because he or she has likely still been influenced by the world's view of dance. Much encouragement may be needed to convince this dancer that the gift is from the Lord. Trust and confidence are best built up through seeking and listening for God's guidance. As you walk in obedience and step out in faith, others will cheer for you along the way. The best place to start learning or relearning is with prayer and the Word.

Pray constantly.
—1 Thessalonians 5:17

Make every effort to present yourself before God as tried
and true, as an unashamed worker cutting a straight
path with the word of truth.
—2 Timothy 2:15

If you enjoy writing, begin journaling about your prayer time with the Lord, keeping track of His guidance and encouragement for you. Make sure to act on the things He speaks to you before trying to move on. If it seems He has gone silent, ask if He is waiting on you or maybe giving you rest.

Know what His Word says about your gift. Become familiar with the scriptures mentioning dance and be able to share them with others. Dancers will often have a specific interest within the dance genres (i.e. praise, worship, intercessory, interpretive, and more). Study the scriptures regarding these subcategories. For example, *Strong's Expanded Exhaustive Concordance of the Bible* lists 248 references to the word *praise*. In studying this one word, you will find that many of the instances using the word *praise* sound like a dance. Some describe exuberant responses while others depict worshipful movements.

Seek out sources to grow in the skill of dance. Whether you've danced before or not, you likely already have some level of natural ability, but the flow of your dance will be greatly helped through lessons. Even professionals continue practicing the basics of dance. Dance lessons can be found through online videos and courses or classes through a Christian dance school. Some questions you might consider before signing up are:

- What is the reputation of the school?

- Are there online reviews?

- What kind, or what style of dance, am I seeking to learn?

- Will the class teach dance as a fun exercise or as a skill?

- Will I be required to participate in recitals or competitions?

- Will a Christian school teach the biblical foundations of dance as well as the technical skills?

Is it important that your source for learning be Christian? I strongly believe so because Christ is the source and foundation of your gift. Your foundation needs to be solid so that your purposes will be pure. Does this mean you should never take lessons from a secular source? This is a personal question that you need to ask the Lord about. Some dancers refuse to return to a secular source, while others will not be harmed by it. While I learned about biblical dance through personal study and online Christian resources, there were no Christian studios in my area. I ended up enrolling in a secular ballet class for adult women. If this is also the only option for you, always keep in mind why you dance (i.e., to glorify the Lord). To avoid any awkward situations, discuss with the instructor ahead of time any requirements for recitals or competitions.

Secular dance can often (but not always) be sensual. Some movements and costumes are just not appropriate for the dancer who desires to dance for the Lord. If the dance or clothing does not bring glory to the Lord, I strongly recommend avoiding it. I do not mean to say that you should never dance unless it is in direct worship to the Lord; weddings and social celebrations are not prohibited in the Bible. Even a competition of skill for the purpose of growth is not wrong. However, the dance genre and clothing must be carefully considered, not only for your sake but also for the sake of any who may choose to follow your example.

...become an example of the faithful—in speech, in conduct,
in love, in faithfulness, and in purity.
—1 Timothy 4:12

As you grow, try to embrace the uniqueness that God has placed in you. Whether you dance solo or in a group, whether you lead in dance or are one of the participants, your gift will not be exactly like another's. Each person is unique, and each dancer at your church or studio moves differently and enjoys different dance expressions. People may have opinions about your style and may even offer suggestions for your improvement, which will likely stem from their own training and experience. Know that they are all well-meaning. Thank them, and take their suggestions to the Lord for His wisdom and direction. Remain open-minded; bless; pray; and, above all, stay in unity and free from offense.

...walk in a manner worthy of the calling to which you were called—with complete humility and gentleness, with patience, putting up with one another in love, making every effort to keep the unity of the Ruach in the bond of shalom.
—Ephesians 4:1–3

– 3 –

The Dance Effect

Yet You are holy, enthroned on
the praises of Israel.
—Psalm 22:4

The power of dance begins with you, that is, your willingness to be the Lord's vessel in ministry. Your dance ministry can be personal, between you and the Lord, or corporate, worshiping with others to the Lord.

Personal ministry occurs when, out of the love in your heart, you desire to honor, bless, and worship the Lord through dance. He delights in receiving your praise, and you know He is with you whenever you dance.

For God Himself has said, "I will never
leave you or forsake you."
—Hebrews 13:5b

Through personal ministry, the Lord will pour out His love upon you as you adore Him. The Holy Spirit may fill you with peace, joy, clarity of mind, wisdom, revelation, physical or emotional healing, or any other good thing He purposes.

The Lord may invite you to dance with or for Him. This often happens to me, especially if I am stressed over too many things to accomplish. He likes to remind me that "only one thing is necessary" (Luke 10:42), that is, being in His presence. I am refreshed and restored in His presence, and He increases my ability to complete my work or accept that it is for another time or day.

I remember one such instance very well. While I was busy working on my tasks, He said clearly, "Come dance with Me."

Now? I thought? *I'm in my shorts and t-shirt, not my dancing clothes!* But I quickly changed my thoughts to, *Yes, Lord.*

He told me to let Him pick the music, which meant I was to hit the "shuffle" icon on my device. I don't remember the first song that played, but it was beautiful and moving. The second song sent me to the floor in tears as I felt His loving presence. After a short time, I was back to my routine with a new attitude and joy in my heart. Don't miss His call to bless you. That is part of the abundant life that Jesus spoke about in John 10:10, and the joy and pleasure written about in Psalm 16:11.

So, what happens when we praise the Lord in corporate dance? In the physical realm, it can bring unity and focus on the One being praised. It has a multiplying effect; when one starts to dance and praise, others become motivated to join in. There is often a tangible change in the atmosphere. Troubles and negative emotions are changed as we shift our focus from earthly problems to the One who holds our lives in His hands.

Psalm 22:4 tells us the Lord is enthroned on, or inhabits, the praises of Israel—Israel being representative of His people (you are also His and therefore included here). That means He dwells in the atmosphere of praise. When you praise the Lord, you have

His attention. You are in His presence, and His presence dispels darkness.

> *Now this is the message we have heard from Him and*
> *announce to you—that God is light and in Him*
> *there is no darkness at all.*
> *—1 John 1:5*

No darkness at all! Why would we not spend time praising Him? Take time to look up and meditate on the following scriptures. Write them out and journal your thoughts. Give Him thanks for all He is and all He gives to those who seek Him. Stop and take in His love toward you. His presence brings strength, joy, and peace (Psalm 29:11, Romans 15:13, Colossians 3:15). His presence brings love (1 John 4:16). In His presence is healing (Psalm 147:3), hope (1 Peter 1:3), and trust (Psalm 37:5, Proverbs 3:5). In His presence is your breakthrough (Psalm 30:12, Psalm 32:7). God's Word, His Holy Bible, is full of promises that are ours, and they come to pass when we spend time in His presence.

> *Enter His gates with thanksgiving and His courts with*
> *praise! Praise Him, bless His Name.*
> *—Psalm 100:4*

> *Then Hezekiah reestablished the divisions of the*
> *kohanim and the Levites together with their divisions,*
> *each of the kohanim and Levites according to his*
> *service: for burnt offerings, peace offerings,*
> *to minister, to praise, or to sing praises in*
> *the gates of the courts of ADONAI.*
> *—2 Chronicles 31:2*

The word *praise* in these verses is *hâlal*, which you may remember means to shine, make a show, boast, be clamorously foolish, rave, and celebrate. Dwell on these verses of *hâlal*, and you will realize that while we enter in with praise, we aren't meant to stand at the entrance. Press in further to the inner courts to worship Him. Our hearts, minds, and lives are changed when we as God's children praise and worship Him in dance. Press in deeply, encourage others to join in, and receive from His hand and heart. By worshiping the Lord so honestly and freely, the move of His presence will affect even those who are not dancing, releasing His blessings on all who will receive.

Through personal and corporate dance you invite the presence of the Lord to move in your midst. The more you praise Him, the closer you become to Him. The closer you relationally come to Him, the more you trust Him. The more you trust Him, the more you will believe Him and see the manifestation of His goodness toward you and in you. There is abundant life waiting for you in Christ Jesus, and it is, in part, released through praise. Praise Him with your dance.

– 4 –

Dancing with Flags and Instruments

The singers go before, the musicians last, between
maidens beating tambourines.
—Psalm 68:26

Worship flags, silk scarves, fans, tambourines and glory hoops, billow cloths, dance streamers, ribbons, and staffs or mattahs are wonderful instruments we can use when worshiping the Lord. Scriptural references can be found for some of these instruments, further deepening the value and meaning of their use in your dance.

Let's look at the use of flags first. We are most familiar with flags as instruments of identification. Representative of their unique designs, flags identify countries, military divisions, states and territories, teams and clubs. They are also decoratively used for seasons, holidays, and personal interests. With God as the Author and Creator of all things, even the idea of the flag comes from Him.

Flags and banners are used throughout the Bible as symbols of identification. They are calls for action, signaling when to gather and when to scatter. As you'll read later in this chapter, banners are also used to identify or represent intimacy and beauty.

Words used in the Bible that signify flags as we know them include standard, ensign, banner, and signal. In Numbers chapters one, two, and ten, flags were used to identify the twelve tribes as they camped and went out by divisions. Here, the Hebrew word for *flag* is *degel* (deh'-gel), which means a flag, banner, or standard. It comes from the word *dagal* (daw-gal'), which means to flaunt, raise a flag, or be conspicuous (to be seen).

In Isaiah and Jeremiah, the Hebrew word for *flag* and *banner* is *nec* (nace), which means a flag or a sail. It usually refers to a flag or sail used as a signal. *Nec* comes from the word *nacac* (naw-sas'), which means to gleam from afar, to be conspicuous, or like a signal. As in the verse below, and throughout Isaiah and Jeremiah, ensigns and banners represent a calling out, a calling to come, an announcement, a drawing of attention, a warning, a powerful signal, a call to station the watchmen, and to blow a shofar.

> *He will lift up a banner to nations far off, and will whistle for them from the ends of the earth. Look!*
> *Swiftly, speedily they come!*
> —Isaiah 5:26

Flags are made and used to be seen, to draw attention. They are used to identify who we are or what we stand for. Are you familiar with the use of flags in a worldly sense, but have difficulty imagining their use in a spiritual or worshipful sense? Let's compare the two, remembering that everything has its origination in the Lord.

As we often see in American history, the uplifting and waving of flags can represent a rallying of the troops. These signals are a motivating reminder of what the troops are contending for or a sign of victory or patriotic resolve. Think of the Fort McHenry

Battle of Baltimore in the War of 1812, the famous photo of soldiers raising the U.S. flag at Iwo Jima during World War II, or the unfurling of the U.S. flag over the Pentagon following the 9/11 attacks. In both the Bible and throughout history, the lifting or waving of flags is also used as signals to advance, warn, or retreat.

Think about representations of our military, parades, and marching bands, half-time shows at football games, or rodeos. What goes before the marching band, group or event? The flags. Flags held high in honor, sometimes as banners held between carriers, or placed on rods and twirled with skill to draw attention. Now think about what (or who) leads or goes ahead of the flags—it's the drum major or majorette carrying or lifting high a staff or baton. There may even be a preceding identifying banner.

Flags, staffs, and banners announce who we are. We might be an army or a band (or an army band for that matter). The powerful use of these instruments draws attention and results in feelings of excitement, expectation, patriotic pride, and joy.

The same things happen when we as dancers and worshipers of our Most High God worship the Lord with flags and various instruments. As with dance, the use of flags can visually draw people's attention to the beauty and conspicuousness of the worship being expressed. Knowing the worship is for the Lord, observers are drawn to focus more intently on Him, as well. Through deeper engagement with the Lord, worldly distractions of the mind disappear. Depending on the dance, rejoicing swells among the people, as love, awe, and peace fill the air. In the habitation of the Lord, all is made well.

Let's briefly look more closely at the banners used in scripture. In the Song of Songs, for example, they depict pictures or symbols of love.

He has brought me to the banquet house
and his banner over me is love.
—Song of Songs 2:4

You are beautiful, my darling, like Tirzah,
lovely as Jerusalem, awesome as an
army with banners.
—Song of Songs 6:4

Who is this that appears like dawn?
As beautiful as the moon, bright as the sun,
awesome as an army with banners.
—Song of Songs 6:10

These beautiful verses represent God's devotion, love, and desire for us. Song of Songs 6:4 compares our beauty to Tirzah and Jerusalem. Tirzah is the name of a city that Joshua conquered (Joshua 11:23, 12:24). It is also the name of one of the daughters of Zelophehad from the tribe of Manasseh, who received an inheritance along with the sons of the twelve tribes (read their interesting story in Numbers 26:33–27:7 and 36:1–13).

Whether Tirzah in this verse refers to a beautiful city or a beautiful daughter, the meaning of the name is most significant: "she is my delight." Throughout scripture, the depth of God's love and mercy for Jerusalem, despite their constant waywardness, is clearly described. One day, our Lord and Savior will reign from the beautiful city in Israel. In Revelation 21:10–27, John describes the beauty of the new Jerusalem, beyond anything we've seen on earth, "coming down out of heaven from God".

Banners mentioned in the Song of Songs 6:4 and 6:10 is from the word *dagal*, which means to flaunt, raise up a flag, and be conspicuous. In verse ten, the bridegroom is declaring the beauty of his bride, comparing her to an army of banners. This is also symbolic of Christ, our Bridegroom, who has the same vision of His precious bride, the Church, the body of Christ.

Are you beginning to see a correlation between the use of flags in the Old Testament and the use of flags and other instruments in our worship today? We can wave our flags and banners as declarations of our devotion to the Lord. We are part of His awesome army, devoted to declaring and ascribing praise to Him. God wants us to be seen. He recognizes us and understands more fully than we do the beautiful instruments we choose to wave in worship, which are reflections of our hearts and minds for Him. He delights in our beauty and in our worship and praise to Him.

Let's look now at the use of tambourines. Psalm 68 is a song written by David for a triumphal procession to the temple, to be joyfully sung as the people went up for celebration and worship.

> *But let the righteous be glad. Let them exult before God.*
> *Let them rejoice with gladness.*
> *—Psalm 68:4*

The Psalm continues to declare God's greatness, His kindness, and His execution of judgment against the enemies of His children. How great He is! The singers led the way. Following them were maidens beating tambourines, and musicians brought up the rear. In Psalm 68:26, I find it interesting that the maidens are mentioned separately from the musicians. This distinction makes me think they were doing more than beating, or playing, an instrument; in their joy, maybe they were also dancing.

Finally, let's consider the use of staffs, or *mattahs* (the feminine Hebraic word for branch, rod, staff, or standard) in worship dance.

Biblically speaking, staffs indicate authority. Beginning in Exodus 4:2–3, the Lord reveals His power and authority when He directs Moses to use the staff in his hand to perform miracles. When Moses throws it down, the staff becomes a snake, and when Moses picks it up, it returns to the form of a staff. God continued to work through Moses' use of the staff to bring plagues of judgment upon Egypt (Exodus 9-10), part the Red Sea to escape from the Egyptians (Exodus 14), cause water to come out of rocks (Exodus 17:5–6), and win a battle against the Amalekites (Exodus 17:8–9).

The Lord caused Aaron's rod, or staff, to bud when it was gathered with the rods of the princes of the other tribes as they had been grumbling against Aaron and his descendants, the priests (Numbers 17:1–10). By causing Aaron's rod to sprout, blossom, and produce almonds, God was showing all of Israel that Aaron and his line were God's chosen ones to serve as priests.

There are many other mentions of rods and staffs within the scriptures. Look for them as you read and study the Bible.

As believers in Christ Jesus, we are a chosen people. Jesus has given us authority over all the power of the enemy. We can certainly praise God in dance using rods and staffs, signifying that He has chosen us, and representing the authority He has given us.

> *But you are a chosen people, a royal priesthood, a holy*
> *nation, a people for God's own possession, so that you*
> *may proclaim the praises of the One who called you out*
> *of darkness into His marvelous light.*
> *—1 Peter 2:9*

> *Behold, I have given you authority to trample upon ser-*
> *pents and scorpions, and over all the power of the*
> *enemy, nothing will harm you.*
> *—Luke 10:19*

I hope this chapter has stirred you to get started or to further grow in dance ministry with flags and other various instruments. They can help draw us into deeper worship and revelation of His goodness toward us. Step out in faith, just as you did with dance. If God is calling you to this ministry, look for local workshops or online videos to become familiar with the instruments. Try different instruments to see what works best for you, keeping in mind where you will use them (indoors, outdoors, large or small spaces, etc.). Mature in your gift from God by studying and practicing. Study scriptures related to flags, rods and staffs, lifting of hands, worship and praise, as well as music and instruments. Allow yourself time to practice, both alone and in a group.

Remember that He gives us gifts, talents, and skills so we can serve Him and draw others to Him. From the parable of talents in Matthew 5:14–30, we can learn that to increase your "talent," you must put it to use. The more we use it for Him, the more He will open up opportunities for growth and ministry. Be led by the Holy Spirit in your ministry. Listen for His voice, and practice His presence.

Are you excited? I'm excited. We can't stay as children. Let's mature in the gifts He has given us for worship and praise. You are part of His kingdom on earth to give Him glory.

– 5 –

Public Ministry

Who may go up on the mountain of ADONAI?
Who may stand in His holy place? One with
clean hands and a pure heart who has not
lifted his soul in vain, nor sworn deceitfully.
—Psalm 24:3–4

In 1 Corinthians 14:26 Paul teaches that when believers come together, each one has a part: a psalm, a teaching, a revelation, or an offering of any other gift to build each other up. While not specifically mentioned in Paul's examples, dance is an acceptable part in building up the Body of Christ. Anytime you offer your gift to the Lord in a church service or other public venue, whether in joint praise and worship or a special dance, you are publicly ministering to the Lord and those around you.

One on one with the Lord, you can dance for Him whenever and however you want. You may simply spend time practicing your skill before Him, maturing in the gift. Maybe you are listening as He gives you His guidance and you visualize a dance to a new song. You can dance in your living room, the closet, the bathroom, the front yard, the back yard, dressed up, or in pajamas. It's just you and the Lord. But how do you prepare for public ministry when others are around and it's no longer just you and the Lord?

The first thing to acknowledge in preparing for public dance ministry for the Lord is the condition of our hearts toward Him. As Psalm 24:3–4 states, when we stand in His holy place, our hands should be clean and our hearts pure. Come before Him in your prayer closet and open yourself up for His loving attention.

Search me, O God, and know my heart. Examine me,
and know my anxious thoughts, and see if
there be any offensive way within me,
and lead me in the way everlasting.
—Psalm 139:23–24

Everyday life can be a challenge, and we need to always be on the alert to things that may negatively affect us. You can likely recall a time when the adversary set out to attack your heart and mind as you were on your way to church or a ministry event. You could have had cross words with a family member, received bad news as you were headed out the door, experienced a crazy driver on the road, or you could have just plain had "stinking thinking."

Take time to give all your frustrations and disappointments to the Lord. Learn to deal with these conflicts immediately, and practice daily to stay free from offense. If something comes along that you can't shake free from, lean on the Lord. He will often give you an answer and the freedom, but you must take the time to search for it and receive it when it's revealed. Don't let your own pride keep you from freedom. It is hard to draw people into the Lord's presence through your ministry if you are visibly struggling yourself. Freedom in the Lord is contagious, but misery doesn't always attract the best company.

Having a clean heart attitude opens you up for the Holy Spirit to work effectively through you and invites unity among other worshipers and leaders. The goal of public ministry is to use the multitude of gifts to 1) glorify and bless the Lord, and 2) reach the multitudes of people. One person's healing, hearing from the Lord, or encouragement from the musicians, may flow from your anointed dance. Others may not be drawn to the Lord by your dance, but during these worship moments the Holy Spirit is more than able to inspire a prophet's voice or an intercessor's prayer that will directly hit the mark in their lives. The gifts are meant to work in unity.

Are you dressed for success? Like it or not, good or bad, how you physically clothe yourself for ministry matters as much as how you spiritually clothe yourself. A few scriptures for inspiration come to mind.

You are to make holy garments for your brother Aaron,
for splendor and for beauty. You are to speak to all
who are skilled, whom I have filled with a spirit
of artistry, to make Aaron's garments for
consecrating him, so that he may
minister to Me as a kohen.
—Exodus 28:2–3

All glorious is the king's daughter within the palace—
her gown is interwoven with gold.
—Psalm 45:14

Let Your kohanim wear righteousness, and let
Your godly ones sing for joy.
—Psalm 132:9

The goal with worship and praise dance clothing is not perfection, but rather, wisdom. Clothing can and should be attractive and beautiful, but its beauty must be honoring to the Lord and enhance the flow of the dance, rather than draw too much attention to the dancer. Again, the above verses are for inspiration and should not be taken as an endorsement of a legalistic view of clothing.

Let's look at three different dances in the Bible in consideration of clothing. When the Israelites had just come through the Red Sea on dry land and observed the sudden destruction of their enemy in mid chase, Moses praised the Lord with song, and Miriam led the women with tambourines and dancing. What was she likely wearing? After traveling and camping for three and a half weeks, she probably was not in her "Sunday best."

When David danced with all his might at the success the Lord gave him in returning the Ark to the City of David, in the manner prescribed by the Lord, he was dressed in his priestly garments created for ministering to the Lord.

What about the spontaneous celebratory dancing at the return of the prodigal son? Upon the prodigal's return, the father told his slaves to quickly bring out the best robe, a ring for his finger and sandals for his feet, kill the fattened calf and celebrate. The older son, returning from work in the fields that same day, was angry that his father had never given him a young goat to celebrate with his friends. So we can see that in a very short time, many had gathered to celebrate and rejoice with music and dancing. Except for the prodigal son, we are not told how the people were dressed. If a neighbor suddenly and excitedly invited you to an impromptu celebration over a child returning home, how would you quickly dress for the celebration? Probably not in clothing you'd been wearing for several days, nor in your "Sunday best," but in something in-between the two.

All three were public dances that brought honor and glory to the Lord, though the dancers' clothing was different in each case. So how do you decide what you should wear? Ask the Lord. Your church may have a specific dress code; if so, honor that. If there is no specific dress code, then always dress to honor the Lord within your circumstances.

At this point, maybe you're thinking, *These points are all great, but my church doesn't allow worship and praise dance. What can I do?* Always first, pray. Ask the Lord to open the hearts and minds of your church's leadership regarding dance. Ask Him for His favor upon you and the wisdom for you to speak with the leadership about introducing worship and praise dance as a ministry to the Lord and His people. Ask questions to find out what the hindrances are, if any: is it unfamiliarity with this kind of ministry or a lack of biblical understanding?

Share this book with your leadership. Allow time for transition. Continue in prayer for your church's leaders, and pray for all areas of their lives and ministry. God is the Creator of dance and is able to turn hearts and minds toward Him. He is also able to move you to a place where you can grow and flourish. Be open to His leading and guidance. He is faithful and trustworthy.

> *Now to Him who is able to do far beyond all that we ask*
> *or imagine, by means of His power that works in us,*
> *to Him be the glory in the community of believers*
> *and in Messiah Yeshua throughout all*
> *generations forever and ever! Amen.*
> *—Ephesians 4:20–21*

– 6 –

Welcoming the Children

"Whoever welcomes one of these children in My name,
welcomes Me; and whoever welcomes Me, welcomes
not Me but the One who sent Me.
—Mark 9:37

Jesus loves the children, all the children of the world. But is there room for them in ministry—dance ministry? Recall from Part One, Chapter 19: The Rejection. Jesus compared that generation to those who would not respond to children calling out or playing joyful or mournful music in the streets. In the leaders' eyes, children were not important. However, in the book of Mark, Jesus reveals that He delights in children.

Jesus exuded wisdom among the people. He healed all who were sick or tormented. He was gentle and humble in spirit and full of love. People began bringing their children to Him, hoping He would touch them with a blessing or a holy anointing. However, the disciples rebuked those who brought the children. They likely thought this wise and important Man should not be bothered with little children.

173

*But when Yeshua saw this, He got angry. He told them,
"Let the little children come to Me! Do not hinder them,
for the kingdom of God belongs to such as these. Amen,
I tell you, whoever does not receive the kingdom
of God like a little child will never enter it!"
—Mark 10:14–15*

Do you feel His heart hurting over their response? He was angry when He spoke the above words to His disciples. Was He angry over the lack of value or the poor treatment of the children? Or angry over them not being allowed to participate in the blessings of Christ? Angry that His disciples thought His blessings were only for select individuals—wasn't that the attitude of the religious leaders that Jesus so often rebuked?

*And He took them in His arms and began blessing them,
laying His hands on them.
—Mark 10:16*

Do you feel His heart of pure and complete love, His willingness to touch and bless? This is how He wants us to treat children. As noted in Psalm 127:3, they are a blessing, a heritage, and a reward from God.

*But Yeshua, knowing the reasoning of their heart, took a
child and set him by His side. He said to them,
"Whoever welcomes this child in My name,
welcomes Me. And whoever welcomes Me,
welcomes the One who sent Me. The one
who is the least among all of you
is the one who is great."
—Luke 9:47–48*

As Jesus' heart is for the children, He deeply desires that all of us believe Him, trust Him, and receive from Him as a child would. So I say, let us receive the children! They look to us as their examples. They desire to be accepted, to be part of the worship, part of our ministry to the Lord and His people. So, let them freely join in worshipful dance. Guide and train them appropriately for their ages. Teach them the scriptures, and include opportunities for them to minister.

I have had the blessing of being part of a smaller church body where we are encouraged to openly grow in the gifts of dance and flag ministry. In fact, we encourage all believers to grow in and use their specific gifts. It is a wonderful place to be when children enter the worship assembly and are obviously so moved by the music and dance that their hearts' desire to join in is written all over their faces. What a blessing and joy it is to welcome them and encourage them in freely praising our Lord.

Larger church bodies may not have similar freedoms for various reasons, but my prayer is that there is a gifting among the people—maybe within you—to teach the children and provide opportunities for them to dance.

Jesus took the little children and blessed them. May we do the same.

– 7 –

Called to Dance
(Personal Testimony)

Here I am, doing a new thing; Now it is springing up—
do you not know about it? I will surely make a way in
the desert, rivers in the wasteland.
—Isaiah 43:19

Sitting quietly in a darkened room filled with Christian women for a weekend retreat, the prophetic psalmist paused between songs. Pointing me out, she said, "This next one's for you." She poured out the Lord's words to me in song: "just like a swan on a lake… like the ripple on the water... like a crystal drop of rain, dancing on the street… dance, child, dance."

Questions raced through my mind. I'd never danced for the Lord before, nor did I have any dance background, so why was she singing these lyrics to me? Did she choose the right person? It was a beautiful song, and I just couldn't get over the fact that it was for me. I bowed my head in my lap, crying as she sang, not understanding what the Lord was saying, but trying to receive that somehow the Lord was pleased with me and giving me a present hope in exchange for hope deferred that had been making my heart sick. For many years, I had been praying and trusting the

Lord for change in difficult personal circumstances, but answers seemed to always elude me.

"...the red seas in life will part... dance a faster dance... just put one foot in front of the other... dance, child, dance." Thinking of the troubles in my life, I decided this must be how I will overcome them, by dancing for the Lord.

During the second night of the retreat, she pointed me out again and declared the Lord was confirming the message. In the Spirit, she saw a clock with the second hand one tick before the midnight hour (think Cinderella and her pumpkin coach). The word was confirmed and the time was very near.

So I began worshiping the Lord, in secret, late at night, in the basement, the music barely audible. With just a few uncomfortable steps, I was often in tears as I tried to move, feeling terribly awkward but worshiping the Lord the best I could. Through these moments, I grieved over my inabilities (not only in dance, but in relationships), and He began to heal my heart from past traumas and current difficulties.

Several years later, I pondered what in the world I was supposed to do with this personal word about dance. I wasn't dancing at church as some had said I would, or anywhere else for that matter. I figured if I was going to do what I had been called to do, I'd better truly learn how to dance. Ballet lessons began but quickly ended due to financial difficulties, so my worship continued, occasionally, in private.

I kept growing in the Lord by reading His Word, praying, and regularly attending church. In the later years of homeschooling my children, a friend spoke to me as we shared a moment of prayer, saying, "I feel the Lord is saying there is something you have 'put on the shelf.' He says it's OK to take it down when the time comes." I wondered if this was about the dance I was called to do, even though I had no clue as to how to get this "something" off the shelf and activated.

A few church changes came over the years. I grew spiritually and enjoyed each one, but I always knew when the Lord was calling me to the next place. Eventually, He led me to a church where the waving of flags and worship dance were welcomed and encouraged. After a year or more with this newest church family, one day the Lord asked if I would wave a banner for Him. With my heart pounding in my chest, and a small portion of boldness barely overcoming the large portion of fear, I picked up a flag, stood on the far side, and waved.

People more confident and more graceful than myself came, waving flags in worship, throughout the church assembly. I would occasionally join in the best I could. Others in my church purchased sets of silk flags. I purchased a set and kept them hidden at home, only to bring them out and wave them during those private alone times with the Lord.

Now, fast forward a few years. A week before the annual women's retreat, guest speakers came to visit my church. They had spent several years ministering in Israel and were now on sabbatical in the United States, spreading God's love and sharing their worship music. They had recorded their music onto several CD albums that were available for purchase. Following the service, I bought three of the CD's and headed to a women's meeting for specific details about our upcoming retreat. We were told that our Sunday service during the retreat would consist of everyone "bringing a part" in accordance with 1 Corinthians 14:26: "What then shall we say, brothers and sisters? When you come together, each of you has a hymn, or a word of instruction, a revelation, a tongue or an interpretation. Everything must be done so that the church may be built up." Fear tried to sneak in. What did I have to offer? I had no idea, but I hoped the Lord would give me something.

Heading home, I popped in one of the new CDs into my car's disc player. Halfway along my route, the fourth song titled, "The Spirit of the Lord," touched me so much that I had to replay it again and again. When I got home, I was thrilled to see that no one was there. I was alone! Practically at a run, I zipped inside, dropped my purse and Bible, grabbed those stashed-away silk flags, and began moving to this song. It was as if the Spirit of the Lord was downloading a dance for me. I was so excited I couldn't stop dancing, and I knew I had my part for the upcoming retreat. With Holy Spirit's help, I slammed the door shut on that spirit of fear.

It was one of the best retreats I've been to as I watched each woman step out and share from the gifts the Lord had placed in her, and I bravely danced the dance. Praise God, something had certainly shifted! I was asked to dance again for the service the following week. I had finally stepped out to put one foot in front of the other.

I am overwhelmed by God's mercy. Sixteen years from His call to the point of stepping out and moving into this anointing seemed like more than "one tick before the midnight hour," but how patient and kind the Lord is, and I am brought to tears as I write this.

Since then, I have continued to grow according to the Lord's direction as I participate in classes, video teachings, and other ministries focused on the biblical study of dancing in worship to the Lord. I love this closing scripture that beautifully describes the emotions my heart feels toward Him and His merciful, glorious ways.

> *O the depth of the riches, both of the wisdom and knowl-edge of God! How unsearchable are His judgments and how incomprehensible His ways! For "who has known the mind of ADONAI, or who has been His counselor?" Or "who has first given to Him, that it shall be repaid to him?" For from Him and through Him and to Him are all things. To Him be the glory forever! Amen.*
> —Romans 11:33–36

– 8 –
Go Dance Your Dance

You are the light of the world. A city set on a hill cannot
be hidden. Neither do people light a lamp and put it
under a basket. Instead, they put it on a lampstand
so it gives light to all in the house. In the same
way, let your light shine before men so they
may see your good works and glorify
your Father in heaven.
—Matthew 5:14–16

As we end our time together, let's ask, "How *did* David dance?" David danced before the Lord with joy, with leaps, with all his might, with shouts, and with the sound of the shofar (2 Samuel 6:12, 14). He followed his dancing with sacrifices and offerings, generous gifts of food for the men and women of Israel, and blessings for his own household (2 Samuel 6:17–20). He danced conspicuously and exuberantly. Let's go in the same style.

My dear dancer, the Lord Himself created dance, and He created you to dance. Maybe you will dance only for Him in the privacy of your home. He delights in that precious time as you minister to and bless Him. Maybe you will dance in church. He so appreciates your heart to freely worship Him, as your freedom also releases others into freedoms of their own. Maybe you will choreograph individual or small-group dances. He rejoices in you using your creativity to bless Him and the congregation. Maybe you will teach dance and put together presentations for larger audiences. It was God's joy to bless you with that ability.

The Lord knows His message will be beautifully spoken through the gift and the artistry of dance. Maybe you will travel the highways, byways, and even to the nations, expressing your love for Him through dance and spreading the Good News of salvation. He is cheering you on to do the things He has called you to do.

And Remember! I am with you always,
even to the end of the age.
—*Matthew 28:20b*

Go, dancer. Dance like David danced.

Appendix

32 DANCE SCRIPTURES

Exodus 15:20
Then Miriam the prophetess, Aaron's sister, took a tambourine in her hand and all the women went out after her with tambourines and with dancing.

Exodus 32:19
Then it happened, as soon as Moses came near the camp, he saw the calf and the dancing, and his anger burned hot. So he threw the tablets out of his hands, and smashed them at the foot of the mountain.

Judges 11:34
Now when Jephthah arrived at his home in Mizpah, behold, his daughter was coming out to meet him with tambourines and with dances. Now she was his only child. Besides her he had no son or daughter.

Judges 21:21
…and watch, and behold, if the daughters of Shiloh should come out to join in the dances, then come out of the vineyards, and let each of you catch his wife from among the daughters of Shiloh. Then go to the land of Benjamin.

Judges 21:23
So the children of Benjamin did so, and took the number of wives from the dancers whom they carried off. Then they went and returned to their inheritance, and rebuilt the towns and settled in them.

1 Samuel 18:6

Upon their coming back, upon David's return from killing the Philistine, the women came out of all the towns of Israel, singing and dancing in circles to greet King Saul, with timbrels, with joy and with three-stringed instruments.

1 Samuel 18:7

So the women sang one to another, as they were dancing saying, "Saul has slain his thousands, and David his ten thousands!"

1 Samuel 21:12

But Achish's courtiers said to him, "Isn't this David king of the land? Isn't he the one they sing about in their dances saying, 'Saul has slain his thousands, and David his ten thousands?'"

1 Samuel 29:5

Isn't this one David, about whom they were singing in dances saying: 'Saul has slain his thousands, and David his ten thousands?'"

1 Samuel 30:16

So he led them down, and behold, they were scattered over all the area, eating, drinking and feasting [dancing] because of all the great spoil that they had taken from the land of the Philistines and from the land of Judah. [brackets added for clarity]

2 Samuel 6:14

Meanwhile, David was dancing before ADONAI with all his might while he was wearing a linen ephod.

2 Samuel 6:16

But as the ark of ADONAI entered the city of David, Saul's daughter Michal looked out of the window and saw King David leaping and dancing before ADONAI, so she despised him in her heart.

1 Samuel 6:21

"It was before ADONAI," David said to Michal, "who chose me instead of your father and all his household, appointing me ruler over the people of ADONAI, over Israel! So I danced before ADONAI..."

1 Kings 18:26

So they took the bull that he gave them, prepared it, and called on the name of Baal from morning till noon, crying, "O Baal, answer us!" But there was no voice—no one was answering. They also danced leaping around the altar that was made.

Isaiah 13:21

But desert creatures will lie there. Their houses will be full of owls. Ostriches will dwell there, and goat-demons will dance there.

Jeremiah 31:4

Again I will build you, so you will be rebuilt, virgin Israel! Again you will take up your tambourines as ornaments, and go out to dances of merrymakers.

Jeremiah 31:13

Then will the virgin rejoice in the dance, both young men and old men together. For I will turn their mourning into joy, and I will comfort them, and make them rejoice out of their sorrow.

Zephaniah 3:17

ADONAI your God is in your midst—a mighty Savior! He will delight over you with joy. He will quiet you with His love. He will dance for joy over you with singing.

Psalm 30:12

You turned my mourning into dancing. You removed my sackcloth and clothed me with joy.

Psalm 87:7

Then singing and dancing—all my fountains of joy are in you!

Psalm 149:3

Let them praise His Name with dancing. Let them sing praises to Him with tambourine and harp.

Psalm 150:4

Praise Him with tambourine and dance. Praise Him with string instruments and flute.

Job 21:11

They send out their little ones like a flock and their children dance.

Song of Songs 7:1

Come back, come back, O Shulammite! Come back, come back, that we may look upon you. Why do you gaze at the Shulammite like the dance of Mahanaim?

Lamentations 5:15

Joy has ceased in our hearts. Our dance has turned into mourning.

Ecclesiastes 3:4

A time to weep and a time to laugh, a time to mourn and a time to dance.

1 Chronicles 15:29

As the Ark of the Covenant of ADONAI came to the City of David, Michal, Saul's daughter, looked out the window. When she saw King David dancing and celebrating, she despised him in her heart.

Matthew 11:17

We played the flute for you, but you did not dance. We wailed, but you did not mourn.

Matthew 14:6

But when Herod's birthday celebration came, the daughter of Herodias danced before them and pleased Herod.

Mark 6:22

When the daughter of Herodias came in and danced, she pleased Herod and those reclining with him. And the king said to the girl, "Ask me for whatever you want, and I'll give it to you!"

Luke 7:32

They are like children sitting in the marketplace and calling to each other, saying, 'We played the flute for you, and you didn't dance. We sang a dirge, and you didn't weep.'

Luke 15:25

Now his older son was out in the field. And as he came near the house, he heard music and dancing.

BIBLICAL DANCES CATEGORIZED

Rejoicing and Praise to God: Exodus 15:20

2 Samuel 6:14, 16, 21

1 Chronicles 15:29

Jeremiah 31:4, 13

Psalm 30:12

Psalm 87:7

Psalm 149:3

Psalm 150:4

Luke 15:25

Community, God-ordained Feast Dances: Judges 21:21, 23

Selfish and Sinful Revelry: Exodus 32:19

1 Samuel 30:16

Victory in War: Judges 11:34

1 Samuel 18:6–7

1 Samuel 21:12

1 Samuel 29:5

**Other Responses to,
or Mentions of, Dance:**

1 Kings 18:26

Job 21:11

Ecclesiastes 3:4

Isaiah 13:21

Lamentations 5:15

Matthew 11:17

Matthew 14:6

Mark 6:22

Luke 7:32

Song of Songs 7:1

**Singing and Dancing
of the Lord:**

Zephaniah 3:17

DEFINITIONS OF DANCE

Hebrew or Aramaic Word	Definition
châgag (khaw-gag′)	to move in a circle, to march in a sacred procession, to observe a festival; to be giddy (celebrate, dance, keep or hold a solemn feast or holiday, reel to and fro)
chûwl (khool) or *chîyl* (kheel)	to twist or whirl in a circular or spiral manner, specifically to dance
kârar (kaw-rar′)	to dance or whirl
mâchôwl (maw-khole′)	a (round) dance, twisting or whirling
mᵉchôlâh (mek-o-law′) (feminine form of *mâchôwl*)	a dance
raqad (raw-kad′)	to stamp, to spring about wildly or for joy

Greek Word	**Definition**
chorós (khor-os')	a ring, round dance (as in a choir round)
orchéomai (or-kheh'-om-ahee)	to dance (from the rank-like or regular motion)

DEFINITIONS OF PRAISE

Hebrew or Aramaic Word	**Definition**
bârak (baw-rak')	to kneel; to bless God (as an act of adoration)
hâlal (haw-lal')	to be clear (of sound, but usually of color); to shine; make a show, boast; be (clamorously) foolish; rave; causatively, to celebrate; to stultify
hillûwl (hil-lool')	a celebration of thanksgiving for harvest (merry, praise)
mahălâl (mah-hal-awl')	fame, praise
shâbach (shaw-bakh')	to address in a loud tone, i.e. (specifically) loud; figuratively, to pacify (as if by words: commend, glory, keep in, praise, still, triumph)
shᵉbach (sheb-akh') (Aramaic)	to adulate, adore, praise

tᵉhillâh (teh-hil-law')	laudation; specifically (concretely) a hymn, praise
tôwdâh (to-daw')	an extension of the hand, (an avowal), or (usually) adoration; (a choir of worshipers, confession, sacrifice of praise, thanksgiving, offering)
yâdâh (yaw-daw')	to use (hold out) the hand; physically, to throw (a stone, an arrow) at or away; especially to revere or worship (with extended hands)
zâmar (zaw-mar')	to play upon a musical instrument; to make music, accompanied by the voice; to celebrate in song and music (give praise, sing forth praises, psalms)

Greek Word	**Definition**
aínesis (ah'-ee-nes-is)	a praising, a thank-offering
ainéō (ahee-neh'-o)	to praise (God)
aînos (ah'-ee-nos)	a story, but used in the sense of praise (of God)

arétē (ar-et'-ay)	manliness (valor), i.e. excellence (intrinsic or attributed praise, virtue)
dóxa (dox'-ah)	glory (as very apparent), dignity, glory(-ious), honour, praise, worship
epainéō (ep-ahee-neh'-o)	to applaud (commend, laud, praise)
épainos (ep'-ahee-nos)	laudation; a commendable thing (praise)
eulogéō (yoo-log-eh'-o)	to speak well of, i.e. (religiously) to bless, praise
hymnéō (hoom-neh'-o)	to sing a hymn or religious ode; to celebrate (God) in song

DEFINITIONS OF REJOICE

Hebrew or Aramaic Word	**Definition**
gîyl (gheel)	to spin round (under the influence of any violent emotion), be glad, joy, be joyful, rejoice
'âlaz (aw-laz')	to jump for joy, exult—be joyful, rejoice, triumph
'âlêz (aw-laze')	exultant, jubilant, rejoicing
'allîyz (al-leez')	exultant, joyous, rejoice(-ing)
'alîytsuth (al-ee-tsooth')	exultation, rejoicing
'âlaç (aw-las')	to leap for joy, exult, wave joyously
'âlats (aw-lats')	to jump for joy, exult—be joyful, rejoice, triumph

sâmach (saw-makh')	to brighten up, gleesome; usually a spontaneous emotion or extreme happiness that is sometimes accompanied by dancing and singing, as at a feast or festival
sâmêach (saw-may'-akh)	blithe or gleeful, joyful, merry-hearted
simchâh (sim-khaw')	blithesomeness or glee, (religious or festival)

Greek Word	**Definition**
agalliáō (ag-al-lee-ah'-o)	to jump for joy, exult, rejoice greatly
synchaírō (soong-khah'-ee-ro)	to sympathize in gladness, congratulate: — rejoice in (with)

GLOSSARY

ADONAI—the LORD

Baal—any of numerous Canaanite and Phoenician local deities

Ben-Elohim—Son of God

Bnei-Yisrael—the children of Israel

Courtiers—royal court companions or advisers

Elohim—God (signifying plurality within the Godhead)

Elyon—God Most High

Halleluyah—Praise God

Kedoshim—saints, holy ones

Kohanim—priests

Kohen—priest

Levite—descendants of the tribe of Levi who served the Temple

Mattah (f.) or Matteh (m.)—branch, rod, staff, standard

Messiah—Anointed One

Ruach—Spirit, breath of God, wind

Ruach ADONAI—Spirit of the Lord

Ruach ha-Kodesh—the Holy Spirit

Shalom—the Hebrew word for *peace,* can also mean *wholeness* or *well-fare*

Shofar—ram's horn

Tabret—a small hand drum, often translated as timbrel or tambourine

Yah—shortened from YHVH or Jehovah, meaning God

Yeshua—Jesus, salvation

Zion—a mountain in Jerusalem, the name is generally used to refer to Jerusalem as a whole or to the land of Israel

Closing Prayer

"I pray not on behalf of these only, but also for those
who believe in Me through their message…"
—John 17:20

Thank you for reading *Dance Like David Danced*. Maybe you picked up this book because you are already ministering to the Lord through dance, or you have a strong desire to, and were looking for a resource to help you grow. I hope these pages have done that for you. I hope you will read *Dance Like David Danced* more than once. Even more important than reading this book, however, is the habit of reading His Book and seeking His face. My prayer is that you have discovered how rich and applicable the Bible is, in and for your life, and that Holy Spirit will stir up a passion in you for His Word and His presence. With God's help, may you live your fullest life in Him.

Possibly, this book is a thing of curiosity that you picked up as you seek whether or not to commit your life to Jesus Christ. For you, I want you to know that He loves you so deeply. Your enemy has been lying to you all your life about who God is; maybe telling you that God doesn't care for you or He would have fixed things by now. Maybe you feel that you've messed up your life so badly that a good God could never accept or love you. Nothing is further from the truth. He has promised that if you seek Him with all your heart, soul, and mind, you will find Him. He is the giver of good gifts, and the lover of your soul.

He has already provided for the forgiveness of all your sins—past, present, and future—by dying for you and all humanity on the cross. It is finished. You only need to turn to Him and receive the gift of salvation that He holds out to you. He has already suffered by taking your sins, and mine. All that is left is to repent of those sins and accept Him as your Savior. You don't need to go to church, or meet with a pastor to do this. You can do this right now, right where you are, just between you and Him. If you would like to receive Him as your Savior, you can pray this simple prayer:

> *Dear Lord Jesus, I recognize and know that I am a sinner. Please forgive me for the wrong things I have done. I want You to be my Savior and Redeemer. I want to now live for You. I accept Your gift of salvation through dying for me on the cross. You are the Way, the Truth and the Life, and I ask You to come into my heart. In Your name I pray, Amen.*

Now ask Him to put new people in your life to encourage and build you up, to grow and be strong in your faith. Seek and enjoy His presence every day through reading His Word, praying, singing, dancing, whatever it is that you would like to offer to Him. He is ready to lead you and guide you in the path He's already planned for you. It may not always be easy, but it will be good.

*"Father, I also want those You have given Me to be with
Me where I am, so that they may see My glory—
the glory You gave Me, for You loved Me
before the foundation of the world."*
—*John 17:24*

… "Yes! I am coming soon!"…
—*Revelation 22:20*

STAY CONNECTED!

Visit DanceLikeDavidDanced.com

Subscribe to Carla J. Perez, Worship on Wings
on YouTube.com

Contact her at
worshiponwings@authorcarlajperez.com

www.ingramcontent.com/pod-product-compliance
Lightning Source LLC
Chambersburg PA
CBHW051519150726
47997CB00001B/306